soups
& stews

soups & stews

MURDOCH BOOKS

Contents

Vegetable
soups

Lentil and silverbeet soup

Chicken stock
1 kg (2 lb 4 oz) chicken trimmings
  (necks, ribs, wings), fat removed
1 small onion, roughly chopped
1 bay leaf
3–4 flat-leaf (Italian) parsley sprigs
1–2 oregano or thyme sprigs

280 g (10 oz/1½ cups) brown lentils,
  washed
850 g (1 lb 12 oz) silverbeet (Swiss
  chard)
60 ml (2 fl oz/¼ cup) olive oil
1 large onion, finely chopped
4 garlic cloves, crushed
35 g (1¼ oz) finely chopped coriander
  (cilantro) leaves
80 ml (2½ fl oz/⅓ cup) lemon juice
lemon wedges, to serve

For the stock, put all the ingredients in a large saucepan, add 3 litres (102 fl oz/12 cups) water and bring to the boil. Skim any scum from the surface. Reduce the heat and simmer for 2 hours. Strain stock, discarding trimmings, onion and herbs. You will need 1 litre (35 fl oz/4 cups) of stock.

Skim any fat from stock. Place lentils in a large saucepan, add stock and 1 litre (35 fl oz/4 cups) water. Bring to the boil, reduce the heat and simmer, covered, for 1 hour.

Meanwhile, remove stems from the silverbeet and shred the leaves. Heat oil in a saucepan over medium heat and cook the onion for 2–3 minutes. Add garlic and cook for 1 minute. Add silverbeet and toss for 2–3 minutes, or until wilted. Stir the mixture into the lentils. Add the coriander and lemon juice, season, and simmer, covered, for 15–20 minutes. Serve with lemon wedges, if you like.

Serves 6

Country-style vegetable soup

225 g (8 oz/1 cup) soup mix or pearl barley
2 teaspoons canola or olive oil
1 large onion, finely chopped
1 green capsicum (pepper), chopped
2 zucchini (courgettes), sliced
2 celery stalks, sliced
125 g (4½ oz/1½ cups) button mushrooms, sliced
2 carrots, sliced
1 orange sweet potato, peeled and chopped
375 g (13 oz/2½ cups) pumpkin, peeled and chopped
2 litres (70 fl oz/8 cups) vegetable stock

Put the soup mix or barley in a large bowl, cover with water and leave to soak for 8 hours, or overnight. Drain and rinse well.

Heat the oil in a large saucepan and cook the onion for 5 minutes, or until soft. Add the capsicum, zucchini, celery and mushrooms and cook for 5 minutes, or until starting to become soft. Add the carrot, sweet potato, pumpkin and soup mix and stir well.

Pour in the stock and bring to the boil. Reduce the heat to low, partially cover the pan with a lid and simmer for 45 minutes, or until the vegetables and soup mix are soft. For a thinner soup add a little water.

Serves 6

Notes: The soup will keep for 2 days in the refrigerator or in the freezer for 1 month. Bring to the boil before serving. Soup mix is a combination of pearl barley, split peas and lentils. Both pearl barley and soup mix are readily available from supermarkets.

Roast pumpkin soup

1.25 kg (2 lb 12 oz) pumpkin (winter
   squash), peeled and cut into chunks
2 tablespoons olive oil
1 large onion, chopped
2 teaspoons ground cumin
1 large carrot, chopped
1 celery stalk, chopped
1 litre (35 fl oz/4 cups) vegetable
   stock
sour cream, finely chopped parsley
   and ground nutmeg, to serve

Preheat the oven to 180°C (350°F/
Gas 4). Put the pumpkin on a greased
baking tray and lightly brush with half
the olive oil. Bake for 25 minutes, or
until softened and slightly browned
around the edges.

Heat the remaining oil in a large
saucepan. Cook the onion and cumin
for 2 minutes, then add the carrot and
celery and cook for 3 minutes more,
stirring frequently. Add the roasted
pumpkin and stock. Bring to the boil,
then reduce the heat and simmer for
20 minutes.

Allow to cool a little, then purée in
batches in a food processor or a
blender. Return soup to the pan and
gently reheat without boiling. Season
to taste with salt and freshly ground
black pepper. Top with sour cream
and sprinkle with chopped parsley
and ground nutmeg.

Serves 6

Note: Butternut pumpkin is often used
in soups as it has a sweeter flavour
than other varieties.

Hint: If the soup is too thick, thin it
down with a little more stock.

Ajo blanco

200 g (7 oz) day-old white crusty
  bread, crusts removed
150 g (5½ oz/1 cup) whole blanched
  almonds
3–4 garlic cloves, chopped
125 ml (4 fl oz/½ cup) extra virgin
  olive oil, plus 2 tablespoons, extra
80 ml (2½ fl oz/⅓ cup) sherry or
  white wine vinegar
350 ml (12 fl oz) vegetable stock
sea salt, to season
80 g (2¾ oz) day-old white crusty
  bread, extra, crusts removed and
  cut into 1 cm (½ inch) cubes
200 g (7 oz) small seedless green
  grapes

Soak the bread in cold water for
5 minutes, then squeeze out any
excess liquid. Put the almonds
and garlic in a food processor and
process until ground. Add the bread
and process until smooth.

With the motor running, add oil in a
steady slow stream until mixture is the
consistency of thick mayonnaise (add
a little water if mixture is too thick).
Slowly add the sherry or vinegar and
325 ml (11 fl oz/1¼ cups) of stock.
Blend for 1 minute. Season with sea
salt. Refrigerate for at least 2 hours.
The soup thickens on refrigeration so
you may need to add stock or water
to thin it.

When ready to serve, heat the extra
oil in a frying pan, add the extra bread
cubes and toss over medium heat for
2–3 minutes, or until golden. Drain on
paper towels. Serve the soup very
cold. Garnish with the grapes and
bread cubes.

Serves 4–6

Leek and potato soup

50 g (1³/₄ oz) butter
1 onion, finely chopped
3 leeks, white part only, chopped
1 celery stalk, finely chopped
1 garlic clove, finely chopped
200 g (7 oz) all-purpose potatoes,
    peeled and chopped
750 ml (26 fl oz/3 cups) chicken stock
220 ml (7³/₄ fl oz) cream (whipping)
2 tablespoons chives, roughly
    chopped
white pepper, to season

Melt butter in a large saucepan and add the onion, leek, celery and garlic. Cover and cook, stirring occasionally, over low heat for 15 minutes, or until the vegetables are softened but not browned. Add the potato and stock and bring to the boil.

Reduce the heat and leave to simmer, covered, for 20 minutes. Allow to cool a little before puréeing in a blender or food processor. Return to the clean saucepan.

Bring the soup gently back to the boil and stir in the cream. Season with the salt and white pepper and then reheat without boiling. Serve hot, or well chilled, garnished with chives.

Serves 4–6

Watercress soup

30 g (1 oz) butter
1 onion, finely chopped
250 g (9 oz) all-purpose potatoes,
   diced
600 ml (21 fl oz) chicken stock
1 kg (2 lb 4 oz) watercress, trimmed
   and chopped
125 ml (4 fl oz/½ cup) cream
125 ml (4 fl oz/½ cup) milk
nutmeg, freshly grated, to season
2 tablespoons chives, roughly
   chopped

Melt butter in a large saucepan and add the onion. Cover and cook over low heat until onion is softened but not browned. Add potato and chicken stock and simmer for 12 minutes, or until the potato is tender. Add the watercress and cook for 1 minute.

Remove from the heat and leave the soup to cool a little before pouring into a blender or food processor. Blend until smooth and return to a clean saucepan.

Bring the soup gently back to the boil and then stir in the cream and the milk. Season with nutmeg, salt and pepper and then reheat without boiling. Serve garnished with chives.

Serves 4

French onion soup

50 g (1³/₄ oz) butter, melted
750 g (1 lb 10 oz/5 cups) onions,
  finely sliced
2 garlic cloves, finely chopped
45 g (1¹/₂ oz/¹/₃ cup) plain (all-
  purpose) flour
2 litres (70 fl oz/8 cups) beef or
  chicken stock
250 ml (9 fl oz/1 cup) white wine
1 dried bay leaf
2 thyme sprigs
8 slices of day-old baguette
100 g (3¹/₂ oz/³/₄ cup) grated gruyère
  cheese

Melt the butter in a large, heavy-bottomed saucepan, then add the onions. Cook onions over low heat for 25 minutes, stirring occasionally, or until they are golden and beginning to caramelise. Add the garlic and flour and stir continuously for 2 minutes.

Stirring, gradually add stock and white wine, then bring to the boil. Reduce the heat, add the bay leaf and thyme, then cover and simmer over medium–low heat for about 25 minutes. Remove the herbs and season to taste.

Preheat the grill (broiler). Toast the baguette slices, divide among four warmed soup bowls then ladle over the soup. Sprinkle with the gruyère cheese, then place bowls under the grill until the cheese melts.

Serves 4

Carrot soup with caraway butter

Caraway butter
1 tablespoon caraway seeds
125 g (4½ oz/½ cup) butter, softened

1 onion, chopped
1 garlic clove, crushed
750 g (1 lb 10 oz) carrots, chopped
1 litre (35 fl oz/4 cups) vegetable
  stock
250 ml (9 fl oz/1 cup) orange juice
rye bread, to serve

To make the butter, dry-fry the caraway seeds in a frying pan over medium heat for 3–4 minutes, or until they start to brown. Leave to cool and then grind in a spice grinder or coffee grinder until fine. Beat the butter and caraway together until smooth. Place in a small square of foil, roll into a log and refrigerate for 30 minutes.

Put the onion, garlic, carrots, stock and orange juice into a saucepan and bring to the boil. Cover and simmer over a low heat for 25 minutes.

Transfer to a blender and blend until smooth. Return to the pan, season to taste and heat through. Cut the butter into 5 mm (¼ inch) thick slices.

Spoon the soup into bowls, top each with two slices of the butter and serve with some rye bread.

Serves 6

Jerusalem artichoke soup

50 g (1³/₄ oz) butter
1 onion, roughly chopped
1 leek, white part only, chopped
1 celery stalk, chopped
2 garlic cloves, chopped
800 g (1 lb 12 oz) jerusalem
   artichokes, cut into 5 cm (2 inch)
   pieces
2 potatoes, about 250 g (9 oz), cut
   into 5 cm (2 inch) pieces
1 teaspoon freshly grated nutmeg
500 ml (17 fl oz/2 cups) chicken stock
   or vegetable stock
500 ml (17 fl oz/2 cups) milk
2 tablespoons finely snipped chives

Heat the butter in a heavy-based saucepan over low heat. Add the onion, leek, celery and garlic and cook for 2 minutes. Cover and simmer, stirring occasionally, for 5 minutes.

Add the jerusalem artichokes, potato and nutmeg and then stir to combine. Cook for 2 minutes, add the stock and 250 ml (9 fl oz/1 cup) of the milk. Bring to the boil, cover and cook for 20 minutes, or until the vegetables are tender.

Remove saucepan from the heat. Using an immersion blender fitted with the chopping blade, whizz soup for 10 seconds, or until it is roughly puréed. Season well with salt and freshly ground black pepper. Stir in remaining milk and half the chives and gently reheat the soup.

Ladle the soup into four bowls and sprinkle with the remaining chives and some freshly ground black pepper.

Serves 4

Bean and barley soup

200 g (7 oz) dried borlotti beans
2 tablespoons olive oil
1 small onion, thinly sliced
2 garlic cloves, crushed
1.5 litres (52 fl oz/6 cups) chicken
  stock
1 tablespoon finely chopped thyme or
  sage
200 g (7 oz) pearl barley
100 g (3½ oz/1 cup) Parmesan
  cheese, grated
1 tablespoon finely chopped parsley
4 teaspoons extra virgin olive oil

Soak the borlotti beans in cold water overnight. Drain off the water and put the beans in a large saucepan with plenty of cold water. Bring to the boil and simmer until tender (this will take about 1½ hours depending on the age of the beans). Drain.

Heat the olive oil in a large saucepan and cook onion over low heat for 6 minutes, or until soft. Season with salt and pepper. Add the garlic and cook without browning for about 20–30 seconds. Add the stock and thyme or sage and bring to the boil.

Stir in the barley a little at a time so that the stock continues to boil, then lower the heat and simmer for 15 minutes. Add the borlotti beans and simmer for 30 minutes, or until the barley is tender.

Puree one-third of soup until smooth, leaving remainder unpuréed to give the soup a little texture. Return to saucepan and stir in the Parmesan and theparsley. Season and stir in 125–250 ml (4–9 fl oz) hot water to give a spoonable consistency. Serve immediately, with a teaspoon of olive oil stirred through each bowl.

Serves 4

Cabbage soup

100 g (3½ oz) dried haricot beans
125 g (4½ oz) bacon, cubed
40 g (1½ oz) butter
1 carrot, sliced
1 onion, chopped
1 leek, white part only, roughly
   chopped
1 turnip, peeled and chopped
bouquet garni
1.25 litres (44 fl oz/5 cups) chicken
   stock
400 g (14 oz) white cabbage, finely
   shredded

Soak beans overnight in cold water. Drain, put in a saucepan and cover with cold water. Bring to the boil and simmer for 5 minutes, then drain. Put bacon in the same saucepan, cover with water and simmer for 5 minutes. Drain and pat dry with kitchen paper.

Melt butter in a large heavy-based saucepan, add bacon and cook for 5 minutes, without browning. Add the beans, carrot, onion, the leek and the turnip and cook for 5 minutes. Add the bouquet garni and chicken stock and bring to the boil. Cover and then simmer for 30 minutes. Add cabbage, uncover and simmer for 30 minutes, or until the beans are tender. Remove the bouquet garni before serving and season to taste.

Serves 4

Potato and pumpkin soup

1 tablespoon canola oil
1 leek, halved lengthways, washed
  and sliced
2 garlic cloves, peeled and crushed
500 g (1 lb 2 oz) white-skinned
  potatoes, peeled and chopped
500 g (1 lb 2 oz) butternut pumpkin
  (squash), peeled, deseeded and
  chopped
1.25 litres (44 fl oz/5 cups) vegetable
  stock
finely chopped fresh chives, to serve
mixed grain bread, to serve

Heat the oil in a large saucepan over medium heat. Add leek and garlic and cook, stirring, for 2 minutes. Reduce the heat to low. Cover the pan with a lid and cook, stirring occasionally, for 7–8 minutes, or until leek is very soft.

Add the potato, pumpkin and stock to the pan. Bring to the boil. Reduce the heat and simmer, partially covered, for 20–25 minutes, or until the vegetables are very soft. Set the pan aside for 10 minutes to allow the mixture to cool slightly.

Purée the soup in a blender or food processor (in batches, if necessary) until smooth. Divide the soup among serving bowls and then sprinkle with chives. Serve with mixed grain bread.

Serves 4

Gazpacho

1 kg (2 lb 4 oz) vine-ripened tomatoes
2 slices day-old white crusty bread,
  crusts removed, broken into pieces
1 red capsicum (pepper), seeded and
  roughly chopped
2 garlic cloves, chopped
1 small green chilli, chopped, optional
1 teaspoon sugar
2 tablespoons red wine vinegar
2 tablespoons extra virgin olive oil

Garnish
½ Lebanese (short) cucumber,
  seeded and finely diced
½ red capsicum (pepper), seeded
  and finely diced
½ green capsicum (pepper), seeded
  and finely diced
½ red onion, finely diced
½ vine-ripened tomato, diced

Score a cross in the base of each tomato. Put in a bowl of boiling water for 10 seconds, then plunge into cold water and peel away the skin from the cross. Cut the tomatoes in half and scoop out the seeds with a teaspoon. Chop the tomato flesh.

Soak the bread in cold water for 5 minutes, then squeeze out any of the excess liquid. Put the bread in a food processor with the tomato, the capsicum, garlic, chilli, sugar and the red wine vinegar and process until combined and smooth.

With motor running, add toil to make a smooth, creamy mixture. Season to taste. Refrigerate for at least 2 hours. Add a little extra vinegar, if desired.

To make the garnish, mix together the ingredients. Spoon the chilled gazpacho into soup bowls, top with a little of the garnish and serve the remaining garnish in separate bowls on the side to add as desired.

Serves 4

Zucchini and basil soup

1 large onion, finely chopped
3 garlic cloves, very finely chopped
½ teaspoon coriander seeds
2 celery stalks, finely diced
6 zucchini (courgettes), roughly diced
3 large waxy potatoes, diced
1.25 litres (44 fl oz/5 cups) chicken
   stock
125 g (4½ oz/½ cup) crème fraîche
   or sour cream
1 large handful basil, torn
2 tablespoons finely chopped flat-leaf
   (Italian) parsley
sea salt, to serve

Put onion, garlic, coriander seeds, celery, zucchini, potato and stock in a large heavy-based saucepan. Bring to the boil over medium heat. Partially cover saucepan and gently simmer for 12–15 minutes, or until all vegetables are cooked through.

Meanwhile, put crème fraîche or sour cream in a small bowl with half of the basil and parsley. Mix together using a fork, then set aside.

Remove saucepan from the heat. Using an immersion blender fitted with the chopping blade, whizz the soup for 20 seconds, or until it is semi-smooth. Stir in the remaining basil. Season with salt and freshly ground black pepper, to taste.

Divide crème fraîche mixture among four bowls, ladle the soup into the bowls and sprinkle with sea salt and freshly ground black pepper. Serve immediately.

Serves 4

Panzanella

1 green capsicum (pepper), halved
and seeded
1 Lebanese (short) cucumber, peeled,
halved and seeded
1/2 small red onion
1 celery stalk
1–2 garlic cloves
410 g (14 1/2 oz) tinned chopped
tomatoes
2 tablespoons tomato paste
(concentrated purée)
250 ml (9 fl oz/1 cup) tomato passata
(puréed tomatoes)
1 1/2 tablespoons white wine vinegar
1 tablespoon olive oil
1 teaspoon soft brown sugar
100 g (3 1/2 oz) stale country-style
white bread, crusts removed
2 tablespoons sliced black olives,
to serve
2 tablespoons baby capers, rinsed
and squeezed dry, to serve
2 tablespoons chopped flat-leaf
(Italian) parsley, to serve

Roughly chop the capsicum, red onion, cucumber, celery and garlic. Combine in a large processor fitted with the metal blade and add the chopped tomatoes and the tomato paste. Whizz for 30 seconds, or until smooth.

Add 250 ml (9 fl oz/1 cup) water, the tomato passata, vinegar, oil and brown sugar. Season well with salt and freshly ground black pepper. Whizz in 3-second bursts for about 20 seconds, or until well combined. Transfer the mixture to a bowl.

Preheat the grill (broiler) to medium. Tear the bread into 2 cm (3/4 inch) chunks, put on a baking tray and toast under the grill until crisp but not browned. Stir the bread through the tomato mixture. Set aside for 15 minutes to allow the flavours to develop. Serve in four bowls topped with the olives, capers and parsley.

Serves 4

Minestrone alla genovese

225 g (8 oz) dried borlotti beans
50 g (1³/₄ oz) lard or butter
1 large onion, finely chopped
1 garlic clove, finely chopped
15 g (¹/₂ oz) parsley, finely chopped
2 sage leaves
100 g (3¹/₂ oz) pancetta, cubed
2 celery stalks, halved then sliced
2 carrots, sliced
3 potatoes, peeled but left whole
1 teaspoon tomato paste
   (concentrated purée)
400 g (14 oz) tinned chopped
   tomatoes
8 basil leaves
3 litres (102 fl oz/12 cups) chicken or
   vegetable stock
2 zucchini (courgettes), sliced
220 g (8 oz) shelled peas
120 g (4¹/₄ oz) runner beans, cut into
   4 cm (1¹/₂ inch) lengths
¹/₄ cabbage, shredded
150 g (5¹/₂ oz) ditalini, avemarie or
   other small pasta
pesto and grated Parmesan cheese,
   to serve

Put the dried beans in a large bowl, cover with cold water and leave to soak overnight. Drain and rinse under cold water.

To make the soffritto, melt the lard in a large saucepan and add the onion, garlic, parsley, sage and pancetta. Cook over low heat, stirring once or twice, for about 10 minutes, or until the onion is soft and golden.

Add the celery, carrot and potatoes and cook for 5 minutes. Stir in the tomato paste, tomatoes, basil and borlotti beans. Season with plenty of pepper. Add the stock and bring slowly to the boil. Cover and leave to simmer for 2 hours, stirring once or twice.

If the potatoes haven't already broken up, roughly break them up with a fork against the side of the pan. Taste for seasoning and add the zucchini, peas, runner beans, cabbage and pasta. Simmer until pasta is al dente. Serve with a dollop of pesto and the Parmesan.

Serves 6

Broad bean soup with a mixed herb paste

1 kg (2 lb 4 oz) broad (fava) beans,
  shelled
2 tablespoons olive oil
2 large leeks, white part only, sliced
1 large onion, chopped
2 celery stalks, sliced
3 garlic cloves, finely chopped
50 g (1³/₄ oz) sliced pancetta, cut into
  matchsticks
1 teaspoon ground cumin
1.25 litres (44 fl oz/5 cups) chicken
  stock or vegetable stock
snipped chives, to serve

Herb paste
1 small handful mint
1 small handful basil
1 small handful flat-leaf (Italian)
  parsley
¹/₂ teaspoon grated lemon zest
1 garlic clove, chopped
2 tablespoons toasted pine nuts
80 ml (2¹/₂ fl oz/¹/₃ cup) olive oil

Soak the broad beans in boiling water for 3–4 minutes, then drain. When cool, slip off the skins.

Gently heat the oil in a heavy-based frying pan over medium heat. Add the leek, onion and celery and sauté for 6 minutes, or until the vegetables are softened. Increase the heat to medium–high, add the garlic, cumin, pancetta and cumin and fry, stirring, for 1 minute.

Transfer the pancetta mixture to a saucepan and add the broad beans and stock. Bring to the boil over medium heat, then reduce the heat and simmer for 10 minutes. Remove the saucepan from the heat. Using an immersion blender fitted with the chopping blade, whizz the soup for 1 minute, or until smooth. Season to taste.

To make the herb paste, put the mint, basil, parsley, lemon zest, garlic and pine nuts in a processor fitted with the metal blade. Whizz until roughly chopped. With the motor running, gradually add the olive oil and whizz for 45–60 seconds.Divide the soup among four bowls and top with the herb paste and chives.

Serves 4

Potato, broccoli and coriander soup

500 g (1 lb 2 oz) broccoli
cooking oil spray
2 onions, finely chopped
2 garlic cloves, finely chopped
2 teaspoons ground cumin
1 teaspoon ground coriander
750 g (1 lb 10 oz) potatoes, cubed
2 small chicken stock (bouillon) cubes
375 ml (13 fl oz/1½ cups) skim milk
3 tablespoons finely chopped
    coriander (cilantro)

Cut the broccoli into small pieces.
Lightly spray the base of a saucepan
with oil, then place over medium heat
and add the onion and the garlic. Add
1 tablespoon of water to prevent any
sticking. Cover and then cook, stirring
very now and again, over low heat for
5 minutes, or until onion has softened
and is lightly golden. Add the ground
cumin and the coriander and cook for
2 minutes.

Add potato and broccoli to the pan,
stir well and add stock cubes and
1 litre (35 fl oz/4 cups) water. Slowly
bring to the boil, reduce the heat,
cover and simmer over low heat for
20 minutes, or until vegetables are
tender. Allow to cool slightly.

Blend soup in batches in a food
processor or blender until smooth.
Return to the pan and stir in milk.
Slowly reheat, without boiling. Stir
chopped coriander through and
season well before serving.

Serves 6

Garlic soup

150 ml (5 fl oz) olive oil
125 g (4½ oz) bacon slices, finely
  chopped
2 bulbs garlic, cloves peeled and
  roughly chopped
1 all-purpose potato, diced
1.5 litres (52 fl oz/6 cups) chicken
  stock
1 bouquet garni
3 egg yolks

Cheese croutons
½ baguette, sliced
50 g (1¾ oz) gruyère cheese, grated

Heat 1 tablespoon of the oil in a large heavy-based saucepan and cook the bacon over medium heat for 5 minutes without browning. Add the garlic and the potato and cook for 5 minutes, or until softened. Add the stock and bouquet garni, bring to the boil and then simmer for 30 minutes, or until the potato starts to dissolve into soup.

Put the egg yolks in a large bowl and pour in remaining oil in a thin stream, whisking until thickened. Gradually whisk in the hot soup. Strain back into saucepan, pressing to extract all liquid, and heat gently without boiling. Season to taste.

To make cheese croutons, preheat the grill (broiler) and lightly toast the bread on both sides. Sprinkle with the cheese and grill until melted. Place a few croutons in each warm bowl and ladle the soup over the top, or serve the croutons on the side.

Serves 4

Hot and sour tofu soup

4 small dried Chinese mushrooms
2 teaspoons vegetable oil
1 teaspoon sesame oil
3 spring onions (scallions), white part
  chopped, greens reserved
2 garlic cloves, crushed
2 teaspoons finely grated fresh ginger
1³/₄ teaspoons ground white pepper
300 g (10½ oz) minced (ground) pork
  or chicken
1.5 litres (52 fl oz/6 cups) salt-
  reduced chicken stock
50 g (1³/₄ oz) drained sliced bamboo
  shoots, cut into thin strips
40 g (1½ oz/¼ cup) drained sliced
  water chestnuts, cut into thin strips
4 tablespoons rice vinegar
1 tablespoon soy sauce
1½ teaspoons chilli garlic sauce
1 teaspoon caster (superfine) sugar
300 g (10½ oz) firm tofu, cut into
  1.5 cm (⁵/₈ inch) dice
1 teaspoon cornflour (cornstarch)
2 eggs, lightly beaten

Soak the mushrooms in hot water for 30 minutes. Drain, reserving about 2 tablespoons of the soaking liquid. Discard mushroom stems and finely slice the caps. Set aside.

Heat the vegetable and sesame oil in a wok over medium–high heat. Add the white part of the spring onions, garlic, ginger and white pepper and stir-fry for 1 minute, or until fragrant. Add pork or chicken and stir-fry, for 3–4 minutes. Add the chicken stock, reserved mushrooms, the bamboo shoots, and the water chestnuts and bring to the boil. Reduce to a simmer and cook, skimming the surface occasionally, for 30 minutes.

Add vinegar, soy, chilli garlic sauce, sugar, and tofu. Combine cornflour with the reserved mushroom soaking liquid until smooth. Stir into the soup and cook for 2 minutes, or until thickened slightly.

Drizzle the beaten eggs onto the top of the soup and leave for 1 minute without stirring, then stir through just before serving. Shred reserved spring onion greens and use to garnish.

Serves 4

Tom yum gai

1.25 litres (44 fl oz/5 cups) good-
  quality chicken stock
4 pieces fresh galangal (about 5 cm/
  2 inches long)
4 kaffir lime leaves, finely shredded
1 lemongrass stem, white part only,
  thickly sliced
4 tablespoons lime juice
3–4 teaspoons fish sauce
2 teaspoons red curry paste
350 g (12 oz) boneless, skinless
  chicken thigh fillets, chopped
1 small red chilli, finely sliced
12 button mushrooms, cut in half
1 handful coriander (cilantro) leaves
1 handful mint
3 spring onions (scallions), finely
  sliced

Bring stock to the boil in a saucepan over high heat. Add tgalangal, kaffir leaves and lemon grass and cook for 8 minutes. Reduce heat and add the lime juice, fish sauce and the curry paste. Stir and simmer for a further 2 minutes.

Add the chicken and cook for about 8 minutes, or until cooked. Remove and set aside. Adjust the taste with a little extra lime juice and fish sauce, if necessary. Strain broth through the muslin (cheesecloth), and discard the pieces. Return broth to the saucepan. Add the chilli, mushrooms and chicken pieces.

Serve the soup topped with herb leaves and spring onions.

Serves 4

Carrot soup with spices

500 g (1 lb 2 oz) carrots
1 brown onion, grated
30 g (1 oz) butter
2 garlic cloves, crushed
1/2 teaspoon ground turmeric
1/2 teaspoon ground ginger
1/2 teaspoon cinnamon
1/2 teaspoon paprika
1/2 teaspoon cumin
pinch of cayenne pepper
1.25 litres (44 fl oz/5 cups) chicken
stock
50 g (1 3/4 oz/1/4 cup) couscous
2 teaspoons lemon juice
chopped flat-leaf (Italian) parsley,
  to garnish

Using the shredding side of a grater, grate the carrots. Place the onion in a saucepan with the butter and cook over medium heat for 3 minutes.

Add garlic, turmeric, ginger, cumin, cinnamon, paprika cayenne pepper and the grated carrot. Cook for a few seconds, then add the chicken stock.

Bring to the boil, cover and reduce to a simmer for 15 minutes. Add the couscous, stir until boiling, then cover and simmer gently for a further 20 minutes. Add the lemon juice and serve hot, topped with a little parsley.

Serves 4

Hearty bean and vegetable soup

1 teaspoon olive oil
100 g (3½ oz) pancetta, trimmed and
  diced
1 leek, thinly sliced
2 garlic cloves, chopped
1 celery stalk, thinly sliced
1 large carrot, diced
2 waxy potatoes, diced
2 litres (70 fl oz/8 cups) chicken stock
400 g (14 oz) tinned chopped
  tomatoes
80 g (2¾ oz/½ cup) macaroni
155 g (5½ oz/1 cup) frozen peas,
  defrosted
1 zucchini (courgette), thinly sliced
185 g (6¼ oz) cauliflower, cut into
  small florets
400 g (14 oz) tinned cannellini (white)
  beans, rinsed and drained
1 handful flat-leaf (Italian) parsley,
  chopped
grated Parmesan cheese, to serve
  (optional)

Heat oil in a large saucepan. Add the pancetta, Ithe eek and the garlic and then cook, stirring, over a low heat for 10 minutes without browning. Add the celery, carrot and potatoes. Cook and stir for a further 5 minutes.

Pour in stock and add the tomatoes. Bring slowly to the boil, then simmer for 15 minutes. Stir in the pasta, peas, zucchini, cauliflower and the beans. Simmer for a further 10 minutes, or until pasta is cooked. Stir in parsley. Serve with grated Pamesan.

Serves 4–6

Notes: You can use red kidney beans instead of cannellini beans, if you prefer. If pancetta is not available you can use 97% fat-free bacon.

Roasted leek and celeriac soup

2 tablespoons olive oil
800 g (1 lb 12 oz/about 2 large) leeks, white part only, cut into 5 cm (2 inch) lengths
1 garlic bulb, unpeeled, halved
800 g (1 lb 12 oz) celeriac, chopped
250 ml (9 fl oz/1 cup) milk
125 ml (4 fl oz/½ cup) thick cream
2 tablespoons snipped chives
slices of toasted baguette, to serve

Preheat the oven to 200°C (400°F/ Gas 6). Put the olive oil in a roasting tin and heat in the oven for 5 minutes.

Add leek and garlic bulb halves and season with salt and freshly ground black pepper. Shake roasting tin to coat the vegetables with oil. Roast for 20–25 minutes, or until leek is tender. Remove the leek and roast garlic for a further 10–15 minutes, or until tender when pierced with the tip of a knife.

Meanwhile, put the celeriac and 750 ml (26 fl oz/3 cups) of water in a large saucepan. Cover and bring to the boil, then reduce the heat to medium–low and simmer for about 20 minutes, or until tender. Add the roasted leek.

Squeeze or scoop the garlic into the saucepan. Season and mix well. Add the milk.

Remove saucepan from the heat. Using an immersion blender fitted with the chopping blade, whizz for 45 seconds, or until puréed. Stir through the cream and then gently reheat soup. Add more milk if soup is too thick. Sprinkle with chives and serve topped with baguette slices.

Serves 4

Beetroot and
red capsicum soup

6 beetroot (beets), 600 g (1 lb 5 oz)
  without stems and leaves
1 tablespoon oil
1 red onion, chopped
1 celery stalk, chopped
1 garlic clove, chopped
1 large red capsicum (pepper),
  seeded and chopped
410 g (14½ oz/1⅔ cups) tinned
  chopped tomatoes
1 tablespoon red wine vinegar
sour cream, to serve
2 tablespoons finely snipped chives,
  to serve

Wearing gloves, peel beetroot with a vegetable peeler and cut it into 3 cm (1¼ inch) dice. Put the beetroot in a saucepan with 1 litre (35 fl oz/4 cups) of water. Slowly bring to the boil over medium–low heat, then reduce the heat and simmer for 25–30 minutes, or until the beetroot is tender. Remove about ½ cup of beetroot cubes, dice and set aside.

Meanwhile, heat the oil in a large heavy-based saucepan over medium heat. Add the onion, celery, garlic and capsicum and stir to coat vegetables in the oil. Reduce heat to low, cover and cook, stirring occasionally, for 10 minutes. Add chopped tomatoes and the vinegar and then simmer for 10 minutes.

Transfer tomato mixture to saucepan containing beetroot and remove pan from the heat. Using an immersion blender fitted with a chopping blade, whizz the soup for 20–30 seconds, or until smooth. Season well.

Ladle soup into four warm bowls and top with a spoonful of sour cream, the reserved diced beetroot and chives.

Serves 4

Spiced pumpkin and lentil soup

1 kg (2 lb 4 oz) pumpkin (squash)
2 tablespoons olive oil
1 large onion, chopped
3 garlic cloves, chopped
1 teaspoon ground turmeric
1/2 teaspoon ground coriander
1/2 teaspoon ground cumin
1/2 teaspoon chilli flakes
135 g (4³/4 oz/1/2 cup) red lentils,
    rinsed and drained
1 litre (35 fl oz/4 cups) boiling water
90 g (3¼ oz/1/3 cup) plain yoghurt,
    to serve

Peel, seed and cube the pumpkin to give 700 g (1 lb 9 oz/4½ cups) of flesh.

Heat the oil in a large saucepan over medium heat. Add the onion and the garlic and fry for 5 minutes, or until softened. Add the turmeric, coriander, cumin and chilli flakes and fry, stirring constantly, for 2 minutes.

Add pumpkin, red lentils and boiling water. Bring to the boil, then reduce the heat and simmer, covered, for 20 minutes, or until the pumpkin and lentils are tender. Set aside to cool for 5 minutes.

Using an immersion blender fitted with the chopping blade, whizz the soup for 25–35 seconds, or until evenly chopped. Season well and reheat the soup.

Ladle the soup into four bowls, top with a spoonful of the yoghurt and sprinkle with freshly ground black pepper.

Serves 4

Minestrone

2 tablespoons olive oil
1 onion, chopped
1 slice rindless bacon, finely chopped
3 carrots, halved lengthways and
  chopped
3 zucchini (courgettes), halved
  lengthways and chopped
2 celery stalks, sliced
2 potatoes, chopped
425 g (15 oz/1^3/$_4$ cups) tinned diced
  tomatoes
300 g (10^1/$_2$ oz/1^1/$_2$ cups) tinned
  4-bean mix, drained and rinsed
30 g (1 oz/^{1}/$_3$ cup) small pasta shapes
125 g (4^1/$_2$ oz/1 cup) green beans,
  trimmed and sliced
grated Parmesan cheese, to serve
chopped parsley, to garnish

Heat oil in a large saucepan and sauté the onion and bacon until the onion is soft. Add the carrot, zucchini, celery, potatoes, tomatoes and 4-bean mix and cook, stirring, for 1 minute.

Add 2.5 litres (87 fl oz/10 cups) water to pan and season with freshly ground black pepper. Bring to the boil, then reduce the heat and simmer, covered, for 1 hour.

Stir in the pasta and green beans and simmer for 12 minutes, or until tender. Sprinkle minestrone with Parmesan cheese, top with parsley and serve with crusty bread.

Serves 8–10

Creamy brussels sprout and leek soup

1 tablespoon olive oil
2 rindless bacon slices, chopped
2 garlic cloves, chopped
3 leeks, white part only, sliced
300 g (10½ oz) brussels sprouts,
  roughly chopped
750 ml (26 fl oz/3 cups) chicken stock
  or vegetable stock
185 ml (6 fl oz/¾ cup) pouring cream
  or milk
slices of toasted crusty bread,
  to serve

Heat the oil in a large saucepan over medium heat. Add chopped bacon and fry for 3 minutes. Add the garlic and leek, cover and fry, stirring often, for a further 5 minutes. Add brussels sprouts, stir to combine, cover and cook, stirring often, for 5 minutes.

Add the stock and season. Bring to the boil, then reduce the heat, cover the pan and simmer for 10 minutes, or until the vegetables are very tender. Set aside to cool for 10 minutes.

Using an immersion blender fitted with chopping blade, whizz soup for 25–30 seconds, or until puréed. Stir through the cream or milk and gently reheat the soup. Serve with slices of toasted crusty bread.

Serves 4

Roasted red capsicum soup

4 large red capsicums (peppers)
4 ripe tomatoes
2 tablespoons oil
1 red onion, chopped
1 garlic clove, crushed
1 litre (35 fl oz/4 cups) vegetable
  stock
1 teaspoon sweet chilli sauce
Parmesan cheese, to serve (optional)

Cut the capsicums into large flat pieces, removing the seeds and membrane. Place skin side up under a hot grill (broiler) until blackened. Leave covered with a dish cloth until cool, then peel away skin and chop the flesh.

Score a small cross in the base of each tomato, put them in a large heatproof bowl and cover with boiling water. Leave for 1 minute, then plunge into cold water and peel the skin from the cross. Cut in half, scoop out the seeds and roughly chop the flesh.

Heat the oil in a large heavy-based saucepan and add the onion. Cook over medium heat for 10 minutes, stirring frequently, until very soft. Add the garlic and cook for a further 1 minute. Add the capsicum, tomato and stock; bring to the boil, reduce the heat and simmer for about 20 minutes.

Purée soup in a food processor or blender until smooth (in batches if necessary). Return to pan to reheat gently and stir in the chilli sauce. If desired, serve topped with shavings of Parmesan.

Serves 6

Chickpea and herb dumpling soup

1 tablespoon oil
1 onion, chopped
2 garlic cloves, crushed
2 teaspoons ground cumin
1 teaspoon ground coriander
¼ teaspoon chilli powder
600 g (1 lb 5 oz) tinned chickpeas, drained
875 ml (28 fl oz/3½ cups) vegetable stock
850 g (1 lb 14 oz) tinned chopped tomatoes
1 tablespoon chopped coriander (cilantro) leaves
125 g (4½ oz/1 cup) self-raising flour
25 g (1 oz) butter, chopped
2 tablespoons grated Parmesan cheese
2 tablespoons mixed chopped herbs, such as chives, flat-leaf (Italian) parsley and coriander (cilantro) leaves
60 ml (2 fl oz/¼ cup) milk

Heat the oil in a large saucepan and cook the onion over medium heat for 2–3 minutes, or until soft. Add the garlic, cumin, ground coriander and chilli, and cook for 1 minute, or until fragrant. Add the chickpeas, stock and tomato. Bring to the boil, then reduce the heat and simmer, covered, for 10 minutes. Stir in the coriander.

To make dumplings, sift the flour into a bowl and add the chopped butter. Rub butter into flour with your fingers until it resembles fine breadcrumbs. Stir in cheese and mixed fresh herbs. Make a well in the centre, add milk and mix until just combined. Bring the dough together into a rough ball, then divide into eight portions and roll into small balls.

Add the dumplings to the soup. Cover and simmer for 20 minutes, or until a skewer comes out clean when inserted into the centre of the dumplings.

Serves 4

Zuppa di verdure

3 tablespoons olive oil
2 small onions, chopped
2 celery stalks, chopped
4 small carrots, chopped
2 large potatoes, diced
2 leeks, sliced
2 garlic cloves, crushed
100 g (3½ oz) runner beans
100 g (3½ oz) shelled green peas
1.75 litres (59 fl oz/7 cups) vegetable
   stock
150 g (5½ oz) cavolo nero or
   cabbage
12 asparagus spears
6 slices country-style bread, such as
   ciabatta, crusts removed
1 garlic clove, cut in half
35 g (1¼ oz/⅓ cup) grated Parmesan
   cheese
extra virgin olive oil, to drizzle

Heat the olive oil in a large saucepan and add onion, celery, carrot, potato, leek and crushed garlic. Cook over low heat for 5–6 minutes, or until the vegetables are softened but not browned. Season, then add 375 ml (13 fl oz/1½ cups) water and bring to the boil. Reduce to low heat and simmer for 30 minutes.

Slice the beans diagonally and add to the pan. Add the peas and stock and simmer for a further 30 minutes. Finely shred the cabbage and slice the asparagus diagonally. Add both to the pan and simmer for a further 5 minutes.

Toast bread and, while still hot, rub on both sides with the cut edge of the halved garlic clove.

Stir Parmesan into the soup and taste for seasoning. Place a slice of toast in the bottom of each bowl and ladle the soup over the top. Drizzle with a little olive oil and serve at once.

Serves 6

Sweet potato, chilli and coriander soup

6 whole coriander (cilantro) plants
  (roots, stems and leaves)
1 small red chilli, seeded and roughly
  chopped
2 garlic cloves, chopped
1 tablespoon oil
1 large onion, chopped
1 celery stalk, chopped
650 g (1 lb 7 oz) orange sweet
  potato, cut into 5 cm (2 inch) pieces
1 litre (35 fl oz/4 cups) chicken stock
  or vegetable stock
145 ml (4³/₄ fl oz) coconut milk

Remove the leaves from the coriander plants. Reserve a few whole leaves for garnishing and chop remainder of the leaves. Set aside. Wash the roots and stems and chop roughly. Put in a mini processor and add the chilli and garlic. Add 2 teaspoons of the oil and whizz for 20 seconds, or until the mixture forms a rough paste.

Heat remaining oil in a large heavy-based saucepan. Add paste and stir over low heat for 2 minutes, or until aromatic. Stir in the onion and celery. Cover and cook for 5 minutes, stirring once or twice.

Add sweet potato and stir to coat. Cook for 2 minutes, then add stock. Bring to the boil, then reduce heat, cover and cook for 20 minutes, or until the sweet potato is tender. Set aside to cool slightly.

Using an immersion blender fitted with chopping blade, whizz soup until smooth. Season well. Stir in coconut milk and gently reheat soup. Add the chopped coriander leaves and serve garnished with the reserved coriander leaves.

Serves 4

Roasted tomato, almond and basil soup

60 ml (2 fl oz/¼ cup) olive oil
1 kg (2 lb 4 oz) large, vine-ripened
  tomatoes
1 large onion, finely chopped
2 garlic cloves, thinly sliced
50 g (1¾ oz/⅓ cup) blanched
  almonds, roughly chopped
2 handfuls basil, roughly torn
750 ml (26 fl oz/3 cups) chicken stock

Preheat the oven to 180°C (350°F/ Gas 4). Grease a baking tray with 1 tablespoon of oil. Cut the tomatoes in half, scoop out seeds and arrange, cut side down, on the prepared tray. Roast for 15 minutes, then remove from the oven and set aside until the tomatoes are cool enough to handle. Discard the tomato skin and roughly chop the flesh.

Heat remaining oil in a large saucepan over medium–low heat. Gently sauté onion and garlic for 5–6 minutes, or until soft and translucent. Add the chopped tomato, almonds and half the basil. Fry, stirring once or twice, for 5 minutes.

Transfer mixture to a small processor fitted with the metal blade and whizz for 15–20 seconds, or until mixture is thick and smooth.

Return the mixture to the saucepan, stir in the stock and bring to the boil over medium–high heat. Stir in the remaining basil, season with salt and freshly ground black pepper, to taste, and serve immediately.

Serves 4

Lentil soup

2 tablespoons olive oil
1 onion, finely chopped
1 leek, finely chopped
4 garlic cloves, finely chopped
1 tablespoon garam masala
1 stick celery, finely diced
1 carrot, finely diced
230 g (8 oz/1¼ cups) brown lentils
400 g (14 oz) tinned chopped
  tomatoes
1 tablespoon tomato paste
  (concentrated purée)
1.75 litres (61 fl oz/7 cups) chicken or
  vegetable stock
2 large sprigs thyme
2 tablespoons chopped parsley,
  to serve
grated Parmesan cheese, to serve

Heat the oil in a large heavy-based saucepan. Add the onion, leek and garlic. Cook and stir for 2 minutes. Add the garam masala and cook for a further 2 minutes. Stir in the celery and carrot. Cover and cook, stirring two or three times, over low heat for 10 minutes, or until the vegetables are softened.

Add lentils and stir to coat in the vegetables. Add the tomatoes, stock, tomato paste and thyme sprigs. Bring to the boil, lower the heat and simmer for 50 minutes, stirring occasionally, or until lentils are tender. If mixture is evaporating too rapidly, add more stock or water to keep lentils covered with liquid. Remove the thyme sprigs. Season well. Serve hot sprinkled with parsley and Parmesan.

Serves 6

Udon noodle and mushroom soup

1.5 litres (52 fl oz/6 cups) vegetable
  stock
2 tablespoons mirin
2 teaspoons grated fresh ginger
1 teaspoon wakame (dried seaweed)
  flakes
150 g (5½ oz) fresh shiitake
  mushrooms, sliced
440 g (15½ oz) packet fresh udon
  noodles
2 spring onions (scallions), sliced
  diagonally
75 g (2½ oz) snow peas (mangetout),
  trimmed and finely sliced
  lengthways
50 g (1¾ oz) bean sprouts, trimmed
2 tablespoons light soy sauce
1 nori sheet, shredded
1 tablespoon shichimi togarashi, for
  sprinkling

Put stock in a large saucepan and bring to the boil. Reduce the heat to a simmer. Add the mirin, ginger, wakame and the sliced mushrooms. Simmer for 5 minutes.

Put the noodles in a large bowl and pour over boiling water. Leave for 1 minute to heat through. Drain, then refresh under cold running water and separate the noodles, then set aside.

Add spring onions, snow peas, bean sprouts, soy sauce and shredded nori to the stock and simmer for a further 2 minutes.

Divide the noodles among four large serving bowls. Ladle over the hot broth and vegetables. Sprinkle with the shichimi togarashi.

Serves 4

Note: Wakame flakes and nori are available from some supermarkets and Asian food stores.

Tomato soup

20 g (³/₄ oz) unsalted butter
1 celery stalk, finely chopped
1 onion, finely chopped
1 carrot, finely chopped
1 garlic clove, crushed
700 g (1 lb 9 oz/2³/₄ cups) tomato-
  based pasta sauce
750 ml (26 fl oz/3 cups) salt-reduced
  chicken or vegetable stock
1 teaspoon sugar
1 parsley sprig
1 bay leaf
250 ml (9 fl oz/1 cup) milk
toast, to serve (optional)

Melt the butter in a saucepan and sauté the celery, onion and carrot for 3–4 minutes. Add garlic and cook for 30 seconds. Add the pasta sauce, chicken or vegetable stock, sugar, parsley sprig and bay leaf. Bring to the boil, then simmer for 10 minutes. Remove the parsley and bay leaf.

Purée soup in a blender, then return it to the pan. Stir through milk and heat until hot. Serve with toast, if you like.

Serves 4

La ribollita

4 tablespoons olive oil
1 onion, finely chopped
1 large carrot
3 celery stalks
2 garlic cloves, crushed
250 g (9 oz) cavolo nero, leaves
   chopped
1 zucchini (courgette), finely chopped
400 g (14 oz) cooked cannellini or
   borlotti beans
400 g (14 oz/2 cups) tinned peeled
   tomatoes
1 whole dried chilli
200 ml (7 fl oz) red wine
1 litre (35 fl oz/4 cups) chicken stock
75 g (2½ oz) stale country-style
   bread, such as ciabatta or pugliese,
   crusts removed and broken into
   2.5 cm (1 inch) pieces
extra virgin olive oil, to serve

Pour the oil into a large saucepan and add the onion. Cook the onion gently over low heat. Finely chop the carrot and celery and add to the pan. Add the garlic, then leave to cook for a few minutes.

Add the zucchini to the pan and cook, stirring occasionally, for 5 minutes, or until vegetables are translucent and have soaked up some of the olive oil. Stir in beans and cook for 5 minutes, then add the tomatoes and chilli and cook for a further 5 minutes to reduce the liquid.

Add the cavolo nero and mix into the soup, stirring until just wilted. Add the wine and stock and gently simmer for about 40 minutes.

Add the bread to the pan. Mix briefly and remove the pan from the heat. Leave for about 30 minutes to rest the soup. Serve hot with a generous drizzle of extra virgin olive oil.

Serves 4

Spinach and lentil soup

250 g (9 oz/1⅓ cups) green lentils, rinsed and picked over
1.5 litres (52 fl oz/6 cups) chicken stock
60 ml (2 fl oz/¼ cup) olive oil
1 large onion, finely chopped
1 fennel bulb, trimmed and finely diced
1 large carrot, finely diced
½ teaspoon fennel seeds
¼ teaspoon cayenne pepper
2 bay leaves
90 g (3¼ oz/⅓ cup) tomato paste (concentrated purée)
3 garlic cloves, halved lengthways and thinly sliced
3 large handfuls baby English spinach, washed
small pinch of sweet smoked paprika
extra virgin olive oil, to serve

Put lentils in a large saucepan and cover with water. Bring to the boil over medium–high heat, then reduce the heat and simmer for 10 minutes. Drain and then return to saucepan. Add the stock and 500 ml (17 fl oz/ 2 cups) of water and bring to the boil. Reduce the heat to medium and simmer for 15 minutes.

Heat 2 tablespoons of oil in a heavy-based frying pan. Add onion, fennel, carrot, cayenne pepper and fennel seeds. Crush the bay leaves and add to the pan. Sauté over low heat for 5 minutes. Stir through tomato paste. Add the onion mixture to the lentils and simmer for about 20 minutes, or until tender.

Gently heat remaining oil in a frying pan over low heat. Add garlic and 2 handfuls of spinach and then cook, stirring, for 2–3 minutes. Add paprika and remaining spinach and simmer for 2 minutes.

Remove the saucepan from the heat and discard the bay leaves. Transfer half the soup to a blender. Whizz for 30 seconds, or until smooth. Return the puréed soup to the saucepan and add the remaining spinach. Season. Drizzle with extra oil.

Serves 4

Ramen noodles with soy broth

Broth

1 kg (2 lb 4 oz) pork bones
1 kg (2 lb 4 oz) chicken bones
10 spring onions (scallions), bruised
10 cm (4 in) piece fresh ginger, sliced
1 bulb garlic, cut in half through
   the centre
2 carrots, peeled and chopped
10 cm (4 in) square piece konbu
   (kelp), wiped with a damp cloth
125–185 ml (4–6 fl oz/$\frac{1}{2}$–$\frac{3}{4}$ cup)
   shoyu (Japanese soy sauce)
80 ml (2$\frac{1}{2}$ fl oz/$\frac{1}{3}$ cup) sake

8 dried shiitake mushrooms
500 g (1 lb 2 oz) fresh ramen noodles
100 g (3$\frac{1}{2}$ oz) bamboo shoots, sliced
125 g (4$\frac{1}{2}$ oz) Chinese barbecued
   pork, sliced
200 g (7 oz) bok choy (pak choy),
   sliced lengthways into wide strips,
   blanched
50 g (1$\frac{3}{4}$ oz) bean sprouts, blanched
4 spring onions (scallions), cut into
   4 cm (1$\frac{1}{2}$ in) lengths

To make broth, put pork and chicken bones in a stockpot and cover with water. Bring to the boil over high heat, then drain. Rinse bones, then return to a stockpot. Add the spring onions, ginger, garlic, carrot and konbu and pour in cold water to cover by about 5 cm (2 in). Bring to the boil over high heat, remove the konbu, then reduce to a simmer. Cook for 6 hours, or until liquid has reduced to about 1.5 litres (52 fl oz/6 cups). Cool slightly, remove bones, then pour the stock through a strainer. Refrigerate for 6 hours, or until cold.

Soak the shiitake in hot water for 30 minutes, then drain. Discard the stems. Bring a saucepan of salted water to the boil, add noodles and separate with chopsticks. Cook for 1–2 minutes. Drain well, then rinse.

Pour broth into a saucepan. Add the shoyu and sake, bring to the boil over high heat, then reduce to a simmer. Pour a little broth into four bowls, then divide the noodles among the bowls. Ladle broth over the noodles. Arrange piles of shiitake, bamboo shoots, bok choy, pork, bean sprouts and spring onion on top of the noodles.

Serves 4

Spicy corn and coconut soup

1 tablespoon oil
1 large onion, chopped
1 celery stalk, chopped
2 garlic cloves, chopped
1 teaspoon ground coriander
1½ teaspoons ground cumin
1–2 teaspoons sambal oelek (see tip)
500 g (1 lb 2 oz) potatoes, chopped
750 ml (26 fl oz/3 cups) chicken stock
  or vegetable stock
420 g (14¾ oz) tinned corn kernels,
  drained
270 ml (9½ fl oz) light coconut milk
1 handful coriander (cilantro) leaves
310 g (11 oz/1¼ cups) tinned
  creamed corn
extra coriander (cilantro) leaves,
  to serve

Heat oil in a heavy-based saucepan over medium–low heat. Add onion, celery and garlic. Stir for 2 minutes to coat the vegetables in the oil. Reduce the heat, cover and simmer, stirring occasionally, for 5 minutes.

Add the ground coriander, cumin and 1 teaspoon of sambal oelek and stir for 1 minute. Add potato and stock. Bring slowly to the boil, then reduce the heat and simmer, covered, for 15 minutes, or until potato is cooked. Stir in corn kernels, coconut milk and the coriander leaves. Set aside to cool slightly.

Using an immersion blender fitted with chopping blade, whizz soup for 20–30 seconds, or until smooth. Stir in creamed corn and gently reheat the soup. Add a little hot water if you prefer a thinner consistency. Season well. Ladle into four bowls and add the remaining sambal oelek, to taste. Sprinkle with extra coriander leaves.

Serves 4

Note: Sambal oelek is available in jars from Asian supermarkets.

Chunky vegetable soup

100 g (3½ oz/½ cup) dried red kidney
  beans or borlotti beans
1 tablespoon olive oil
1 leek, halved lengthways, chopped
1 small onion, diced
2 carrots, chopped
2 celery sticks, chopped
1 large zucchini (courgette), chopped
1 tablespoon tomato paste
  (concentrated purée)
1 litre (35 fl oz/4 cups) vegetable
  stock
400 g (14 oz) pumpkin, cut into 2 cm
  (¾ inch) cubes
2 potatoes, cut into 2 cm (¾ inch)
  cubes
7 g (¼ oz) chopped flat-leaf (Italian)
  parsley

Put the beans in a large bowl, cover
with cold water and soak overnight.
Rinse, then transfer to a saucepan,
cover with cold water and cook for
45 minutes, or until just tender. Drain.

Meanwhile, heat the oil in a saucepan.
Add the leek and the onion, and cook
over medium heat for 2–3 minutes.
Add the carrot, celery and zucchini,
and cook for 3–4 minutes. Add the
tomato paste and stir for a 1 minute.
Pour in stock and 1.25 litres (44 fl oz/
5 cups) water, and bring to the boil.
Reduce the heat to low and simmer
for 20 minutes.

Add pumpkin, potato, parsley and red
kidney beans, and then simmer for a
further 20 minutes, or until vegetables
are tender and the beans are cooked.
Season to taste. Serve immediately
with crusty bread.

Serves 6

Barley soup with golden parsnips

200 g (7 oz) pearl barley
1 tablespoon oil
2 onions, chopped
2 garlic cloves, finely chopped
2 carrots, chopped
2 potatoes, chopped
2 celery sticks, chopped
2 bay leaves, torn in half
2 litres (70 fl oz/8 cups) chicken stock
125 ml (4 fl oz/1/2 cup) milk
40 g (11/2 oz) butter
3 parsnips, cubed
1 teaspoon soft brown sugar
chopped parsley, to serve

Soak the barley in water overnight. Drain. Place in a saucepan with 2 litres water. Bring to the boil, then reduce the heat and simmer, partially covered, for 11/4 hours, or until tender. Drain the barley.

Heat the oil in a large saucepan, add the onion, garlic, carrot, potato and celery, and cook for 3 minutes. Stir well and cook, covered, for 15 minutes over low heat, stirring.

Add barley, bay leaves, stock, milk, 2 teaspoons of salt and 1 teaspoon of pepper. Bring to the boil, then reduce the heat and simmer soup, partially covered, for 35 minutes. If soup is too thick, add about 250 ml (9 fl oz/1 cup) cold water, a little at a time, until soup reaches your preferred consistency.

While soup is simmering, melt butter in a frying pan, add parsnip and toss in the butter. Sprinkle with sugar and cook until golden brown and tender. Serve the parsnip on top of the soup and sprinkle with the parsley.

Serves 6

Sweet potato soup

1 tablespoon vegetable oil
1 large onion, chopped
4 garlic cloves, crushed
2 teaspoons grated fresh ginger
1 tablespoon madras curry powder
1 kg (2 lb 4 oz) orange sweet potato,
   peeled and chopped into 5 cm
   (2 inch) chunks
1 litre (35 fl oz/4 cups) vegetable or
   chicken stock
400 g (14 oz) coconut milk
1 small handful coriander (cilantro)
   leaves, chopped
fried Asian shallots and naan bread or
   chappati, to serve

Heat the oil in a large saucepan. Add the onion and cook over medium heat for 3 minutes, or until softened. Add garlic, ginger and curry powder. Stir for a further 1 minute. Add sweet potato and stir to coat in the mixture.

Pour over the stock. Bring to the boil then lower heat. Cover and simmer for 20 minutes, or until sweet potato is cooked.

Cool slightly, then process in batches, using a food processor, until smooth. Return to the saucepan and stir in the coconut milk and coriander, reserving some coriander for garnish. Stir and reheat for 2–3 minutes. Serve in the bowls topped with a sprinkle of fried Asian shallots and coriander. Serve with heated naan bread or chappati.

Serves 4

Note: Fried onion flakes are available from Asian food stores.

Pappa al pomodoro

900 g (2 lb) very ripe tomatoes or
800 g (1 lb 2 oz) tinned chopped
   tomatoes
3 tablespoons olive oil
3 garlic cloves, finely sliced
200 g (7 oz) stale country-style bread,
   such as ciabatta or pugliese, crusts
   removed
15 g (½ oz) basil, torn into large
   pieces
50 ml (1¾ fl oz) extra virgin olive oil,
   plus extra to serve

If using fresh tomatoes, remove stems and score a cross in the bottom of each one. Blanch in boiling water for 30 seconds. Transfer to cold water, then peel the skin away from cross (it should slip off fairly easily) and chop the tomatoes.

Pour the olive oil into a large heavy-based saucepan, add the garlic and cook gently until light golden brown. Add the tomatoes, taking care as the oil may spit. Season.

Bring the tomatoes to the boil and gently simmer, stirring occasionally so they don't stick. Simmer for about 10 minutes, stirring more frequently, until the mixture has thickened.

Break the bread into chunks and add to the pan. Remove from the heat and stir briefly to coat the bread with the tomato mixture. Scatter with the basil, season and pour 500 ml (17 fl oz/2 cups) boiling water over the bread. Add the olive oil and stir a little, being careful not to break up the bread too much.

Leave to rest for 5 minutes before serving. Serve in hot bowls with an extra drizzle of oil on top.

Serves 8

Soupe au pistou

250 g (9 oz) dried haricot beans
2 teaspoons olive oil
1 onion, finely chopped
2 garlic cloves, crushed
1 stalk celery, chopped
3 carrots, diced
1 bouquet garni
4 all-purpose potatoes, diced
150 g (5½ oz) small green beans,
   chopped
500 ml (17 fl oz/2 cups) chicken stock
3 tomatoes
4 zucchini (courgettes), diced
150 g (5½ oz) vermicelli noodles,
   broken into pieces
150 g (5½ oz) peas, fresh or frozen

Pistou
6 garlic cloves, peeled and chopped
80 g (2¾ oz) basil
100 g (3½ oz) Parmesan cheese,
   grated
200 ml (7 fl oz) olive oil

Soak the haricot beans in cold water overnight. Drain, place in a saucepan, then and cover with cold water. Bring to the boil, then lower the heat and simmer for 1 hour, or until beans are tender. Drain well.

To make the pistou, put garlic, basil and Parmesan in a food processor and process until finely ground. Add the oil in a thin stream with the motor running. Mix. Cover with plastic wrap and set aside.

Heat the olive oil in a saucepan. Add onion and garlic and cook over low heat for 5 minutes. Add celery, carrot and the bouquet garni and cook for 10 minutes, stirring. Add the potato, green beans, the chicken stock and 1.75 litres (61 fl oz/7 cups) water and simmer for 10 minutes.

Score a cross in the base of each tomato. Plunge into boiling water for 20 seconds, then drain and peel the skin away from the cross. Chop the tomatoes finely, discarding the cores. Add to soup with the zucchini, haricot beans, vermicelli and peas. Cook for 10 minutes or until tender. Season and then serve with pistou spooned on the top.

Serves 4

Pasta and bean soup

200 g (7 oz) dried borlotti beans
60 ml (2 fl oz/¼ cup) olive oil
90 g (3¼ oz) piece pancetta, finely
  diced
1 onion, finely chopped
2 garlic cloves, crushed
1 celery stick, thinly sliced
1 carrot, diced
1 bay leaf
1 sprig rosemary
1 sprig flat-leaf (Italian) parsley
400 g (14 oz) tinned diced tomatoes,
  drained
1.6 litres (55 fl oz) vegetable stock
2 tablespoons finely chopped flat-leaf
  (Italian) parsley
150 g (5½ oz) ditalini or other small
  dried pasta
extra virgin olive oil, to serve
grated Parmesan cheese, to serve

Place beans in a large bowl, cover with cold water and leave to soak overnight. Drain and rinse.

Heat oil in a large saucepan, add the pancetta, onion, garlic, celery and the carrot, and cook over medium heat for 5 minutes, or until golden. Season with pepper. Add rosemary, parsley, tomato, stock, beans and the bay leaf and bring to the boil. Reduce the heat and simmer for 1½ hours, or until the beans are tender. Add more boiling water if required to maintain the level of the liquid.

Discard the bay leaf, rosemary and the parsley sprigs. Scoop out 250 ml (9 fl oz/1 cup) of bean mixture and purée in a food processor or blender. Return to the pan, season, and then add the parsley and pasta. Simmer for 6 minutes, or until the pasta is al dente. Remove from the heat and set aside for 10 minutes. Serve drizzled with extra virgin olive oil and sprinkled with Parmesan.

Serves 4

Split pea and sweet potato soup

80 ml (2½ fl oz/⅓ cup) olive oil
1 large onion, chopped
2 garlic cloves, finely chopped
2 teaspoons finely chopped fresh
  ginger
120 g (4¼ oz/½ cup) yellow split
  peas
1 red chilli, seeded and sliced
½ teaspoon sweet smoked paprika
1 litre (35 fl oz/4 cups) chicken stock
500 g (1 lb 2 oz) orange sweet
  potato, cubed
1 tablespoon finely chopped mint

Heat 1 tablespoon of the oil in a large saucepan over medium heat. Fry the onion, the garlic and the ginger for 4–5 minutes, or until soft and golden. Stir in the split peas, chilli and paprika and cook for 1 minute. Add the stock and bring to the boil. Reduce the heat and simmer for 20 minutes.

Add the sweet potato, return to the boil, then reduce the heat and simmer for 15 minutes, or until sweet potato is tender.

Meanwhile, heat the remaining oil in a small saucepan over low heat. Stir in the mint, then immediately remove the saucepan from the heat. Transfer the mint and oil to a small dish.

Remove the soup from the heat. Using an immersion blender fitted with the chopping blade, whizz for 30 seconds, or until puréed.

Ladle the soup into four bowls and drizzle with a little of the minted oil.

Serves 4

Chilled cucumber yoghurt soup

2 telegraph (long) cucumbers, about
  550 g (1 lb 4 oz)
1 large handful mint
2 garlic cloves, chopped
1 teaspoon dried mint
125 ml (4 fl oz/½ cup) milk
500 g (1 lb 2 oz/2 cups) Greek-style
  yoghurt
2–3 teaspoons lemon juice, to taste
3–4 drops Tabasco sauce, to taste
2 tablespoons finely snipped chives,
  to serve

Peel the cucumbers, halve them lengthways and scoop out the seeds. Set aside about one-third of one of the cucumbers.

Put the remaining cucumber in a small processor fitted with the metal blade. Add the mint, garlic, dried mint and milk and whizz in 3–4 second bursts for 20 seconds. Add the yoghurt, and the lemon juice and Tabasco sauce to taste, and season well with salt and black pepper. Whizz until smooth and well combined. Transfer soup to a bowl, cover and refrigerate for at least 2 hours to allow flavours to develop.

Finely dice the reserved cucumber. Ladle soup into bowls and top with the diced cucumber and chives.

Serves 4

Note: The soup should be consumed within 1 day.

Vegetable
stews

Autumn vegetable stew

185 g (6½ oz) frozen broad beans, thawed
150 g (5½ oz) baby onions
50 g (1¾ oz) butter
2 teaspoons olive oil
400 g (14 oz) small parsnips
150 g (5½ oz) Jerusalem artichokes
2 tablespoons plain (all-purpose) flour
580 ml (20¼ fl oz/2⅓ cups) chicken stock
300 ml (10½ fl oz) cream
2 teaspoons grated lemon zest
1 teaspoon grated orange zest
400 g (14 oz) baby carrots, trimmed
500 g (1 lb) baby turnips, trimmed

Peel and discard tough outer skin of the broad beans. Carefully peel the onions, leaving flat root end attached, then cut a cross through the root end of each onion.

Heat butter and oil in a large, heavy-based saucepan until foamy. Add the onions and cook for about 7 minutes over low–medium heat, turning often to colour evenly.

While the onions are browning, peel the parsnips and artichokes, and cut them into bite-size pieces. Add to the saucepan and toss well. Scatter flour over onion, parsnip and artichokes, toss to coat and cook for 2 minutes.

Stir in the chicken stock, cream, lemon zest and orange zest. Bring to the boil, stirring, then reduce the heat and simmer for 7 minutes, or until the vegetables are half-cooked.

Add the carrots and turnips, and toss well. Cover the pan and cook for 4–5 minutes, or until the vegetables are just tender. Season well, stir in the peeled broad beans to heat through, and serve.

Serves 4–6

Dhal with vegetables

150 g (5½ oz/²/₃ cup) yellow lentils
150 g (5½ oz/²/₃ cup) red lentils
1 tablespoon ghee
1 onion, chopped
2 garlic cloves, crushed
1 tablespoon fenugreek seeds
2 teaspoons ground cumin
2 teaspoons ground coriander
½ teaspoon ground turmeric
400 g (14 oz) tinned chopped
  tomatoes
750 ml (26 fl oz/3 cups) vegetable
  stock
2 carrots, chopped
250 g (9 oz) cauliflower florets
150 g (5½ oz) green beans, trimmed
  and halved
3 tablespoons cream (whipping)
2 tablespoons chopped coriander
  (cilantro) leaves
naan bread, to serve

Rinse the lentils, separately, under cold water until the water runs clear, then drain well. Put the yellow lentils in a small bowl, cover with water and stand for 30 minutes, then drain well.

Heat the ghee in a saucepan over medium heat. Cook onion and garlic, stirring, for about 3 minutes, or until the onion is soft.

Stir in spices and cook, stirring, for about 30 seconds, or until fragrant. Add the lentils, tomatoes and stock. Bring to the boil over high heat, then reduce the heat to low and simmer, covered, for 20 minutes.

Stir in carrots and cauliflower. Cover and cook for 10 minutes. Add the beans and then cook, covered, for a further 5 minutes, or until lentils are tender and vegetables are cooked. Season to taste. Stir in cream. Serve the dhal sprinkled with coriander leaves and serve with naan bread.

Serves 6

Pumpkin and sweet potato stew

60 g (2¼ oz) butter
1 large brown onion, finely chopped
2 garlic cloves, finely chopped
1 teaspoon ground ginger
1 teaspoon ground turmeric
1 cinnamon stick
pinch of cayenne pepper, or
  ½ teaspoon harissa, or to taste
500 ml (17 fl oz/2 cups) vegetable or
  chicken stock
⅛ teaspoon ground saffron threads
600 g (1 lb 5 oz) butternut pumpkin
  (squash) or other firm pumpkin
  (winter squash), peeled and cubed
500 g (1 lb 2 oz) orange sweet
  potato, peeled and cubed
60 g (2¼ oz/½ cup) raisins
1 tablespoon honey
coriander (cilantro) leaves, to serve

Melt the butter in a saucepan over low heat. Add the onion and cook gently, stirring for 5 minutes, until softened. Add the garlic, the ginger, turmeric, the cinnamon stick and the cayenne pepper or the harissa. Stir over low heat for 1–2 minutes or until fragrant. Pour in tstock, add the saffron, then increase the heat to medium and bring to the boil.

Add pumpkin, sweet potato, raisins and honey and season. Cover and simmer for a further 15 minutes, or until vegetables are tender. Remove cinnamon stick, transfer vegetables to a bowl and scatter the stew with coriander leaves.

Serves 4–6

Tomato and potato stew

3 tablespoons olive oil
2 red capsicums (peppers), chopped
2 green capsicums (peppers),
    chopped
3 onions, thinly sliced
4 garlic cloves, crushed
800 g (1 lb 12 oz) tinned chopped
    tomatoes
3–4 thyme sprigs, plus extra,
    to garnish
2 bay leaves
2 teaspoons caster (superfine) sugar
1.2 kg (2 lb 7 oz) potatoes, cut into
    chunks
125 g (4½ oz/1 cup) black olives,
    pitted
Parmesan cheese shavings, to serve

Heat the oil in a large, heavy-based saucepan. When the oil is hot, cook the capsicum, onion and garlic over medium heat for 10 minutes, or until softened. Add the chopped tomatoes, 125 ml (4 fl oz/½ cup) water, thyme sprigs, bay leaves and sugar. Season with salt and freshly ground black pepper to taste and leave to simmer gently for 15 minutes.

Add potato chunks, cover and cook very gently for about an hour, or until tender. Stir in olives. Garnish with the Parmesan shavings and thyme sprigs.

Serves 6

Bean and capsicum stew

200 g (7 oz/1 cup) dried haricot
beans (see note)
2 tablespoons olive oil
2 large garlic cloves, crushed
1 red onion, halved and cut into
thin wedges
1 red capsicum (pepper), cut into
squares
1 green capsicum (pepper), cut into
squares
800 g (1 lb 12 oz) tinned chopped
tomatoes
2 tablespoons tomato paste
(concentrated purée)
500 ml (17 fl oz/2 cups) vegetable
stock
2 tablespoons chopped basil
125 g (4½ oz/²/₃ cup) kalamata
olives, pitted
1–2 teaspoons soft brown sugar

Put beans in a large bowl, cover with
cold water and soak overnight. Rinse
well, transfer to a saucepan, cover
with water and cook for 45 minutes,
or until just tender. Drain.

Heat oil in a large saucepan. Cook
garlic and onion over medium heat
for 2–3 minutes, or until onion is soft.
Add the red and green capsicums
and cook for a further 5 minutes.

Stir in tomato, tomato paste, stock
and the beans. Simmer, covered, for
40 minutes, or until beans are cooked
through. Stir in basil, olives and sugar.
Season. Serve hot with crusty bread.

Serves 4–6

Spicy vegetable stew with dhal

Dhal
165 g (5³/₄ oz) yellow split peas
5 cm (2 inch) piece of fresh ginger,
  grated
2–3 garlic cloves, crushed
1 red chilli, seeded and chopped

3 tomatoes
2 tablespoons oil
1 teaspoon yellow mustard seeds
1 teaspoon cumin seeds
1 teaspoon ground cumin
¹/₂ teaspoon garam masala
1 red onion, cut into thin wedges
3 slender eggplants (aubergines),
  thickly sliced
2 carrots, thickly sliced
¹/₂ cauliflower, cut into florets
375 ml (13 fl oz/1¹/₂ cups) vegetable
  stock
2 small zucchini (courgettes), thickly
  sliced
90 g (3¹/₄ oz/¹/₂ cup) frozen peas
1 large handful coriander (cilantro)
  leaves

To make the dhal, put split peas in a bowl, cover with water and soak for 2 hours. Drain. Place in a saucepan with ginger, garlic, chilli and 750 ml (26 fl oz/3 cups) water. Bring to the boil, reduce the heat and simmer for 45 minutes, or until soft.

Score a cross in the base of each tomato, soak in boiling water for 30 seconds, then plunge into cold water and peel skin away from the cross. Cut in half and scoop out seeds with a teaspoon. Chop the tomato flesh.

Heat oil in a large saucepan. Cook the spices over medium heat for 30 seconds, or until fragrant. Add tonion and cook for 2 minutes, or until onion is soft. Stir in the tomato, eggplant, carrot and cauliflower.

Add dhal and stock, mix together and simmer, covered, for 45 minutes, or until the vegetables are tender. Stir occasionally. Add zucchini and peas during the last 10 minutes of cooking. Stir in coriander leaves and serve hot.

Serves 4–6

Spicy chickpea and vegetable casserole

330 g (10½ oz/1½ cups) dried
  chickpeas
2 tablespoons olive oil
1 large onion, chopped
1 garlic clove, crushed
3 teaspoons ground cumin
½ teaspoon chilli powder
½ teaspoon allspice
400 g (14 oz) tinned chopped
  tomatoes
375 ml (13 fl oz/1½ cups) vegetable
  stock
300 g (10½ oz) pumpkin (winter
  squash), peeled and cut into
  large dice
150 g (5½ oz) green beans, trimmed
200 g (7 oz) baby (pattypan) squash,
  quartered
2 tablespoons tomato paste
  (concentrated purée)
1 teaspoon dried oregano

Soak the chickpeas in enough cold water to cover overnight. Drain.

Heat olive oil in a large saucepan. Add the onion and garlic and sauté for 3 minutes, or until softened. Add the cumin, chilli powder and allspice and cook, stirring, for 1 minute. Add chickpeas, tomato and stock. Bring to the boil, reduce the heat, cover and simmer for 1 hour, stirring every now and then.

Stir in the pumpkin, beans, squash, the tomato paste and the oregano. Cover and simmer for 15 minutes, then remove the lid and simmer for 10 minutes to reduce and thicken sauce slightly. Serve hot.

Serves 4

Note: A quick way to soak chickpeas is to place them in a large saucepan, cover with cold water, bring to the boil, then remove from the heat and leave to soak for 2 hours. If you're in a hurry, use tinned chickpeas—drain and rinse thoroughly before use.

Lentil bhuja casserole

375 g (13 oz/2 cups) green lentils
1 large onion
1 large all-purpose potato
1 teaspoon ground cumin
1 teaspoon ground coriander
1 teaspoon ground turmeric
90 g (3¼ oz/¾ cup) plain
  (all-purpose) flour
vegetable oil, for pan-frying
2 garlic cloves, crushed
1 tablespoon grated fresh ginger
250 ml (9 fl oz/1 cup) tomato passata
  (puréed tomatoes)
500 ml (17 fl oz/2 cups) vegetable
  stock
250 ml (9 fl oz/1 cup) cream
200 g (7 oz) green beans, trimmed
2 carrots, sliced
pitta bread, to serve

Put lentils in a bowl, cover with cold water and leave to soak overnight. Drain well and place in a bowl.

Grate onion and potato, place in a clean tea towel (dish towel) and squeeze out excess moisture. Add to the lentils with spices and flour and mix well. Using dry hands, roll the mixture into walnut-sized balls and place on a foil-lined tray. Cover and refrigerate for 30 minutes.

Heat about 2 cm (¾ inch) of oil in a heavy-based frying pan. Add the lentil balls in small batches and fry over high heat for 5 minutes, or until lentils are golden brown. Drain on paper towels.

Heat another 2 tablespoons oil in a large saucepan. Add the garlic and ginger and sauté over medium heat for 1 minute, then stir in the tomato passata, stock and cream. Bring to the boil, then reduce the heat and simmer for 10 minutes.

Add the lentil balls, beans and carrot. Cover and simmer for 35 minutes, stirring occasionally. Serve hot, with pitta bread.

Serves 4–6

Fennel, tomato and white bean stew

5 ripe tomatoes
2 leeks, white part only, sliced
2 garlic cloves, finely chopped
1 large fennel bulb, washed, halved, cored and sliced
60 ml (2 fl oz/¼ cup) extra virgin olive oil
60 ml (2 fl oz/¼ cup) Pernod
2 bay leaves
5 thyme sprigs
500 g (1 lb 2 oz) all-purpose potatoes, peeled and cut into large chunks
400 g (14 oz) tinned cannellini beans, rinsed and drained
250 ml (9 fl oz/1 cup) vegetable stock
250 ml (9 fl oz/1 cup) dry white wine
ready-made pesto, to serve

Preheat the oven to 180°C (350°F/ Gas 4). Score a cross in base of each tomato. Place in a heatproof bowl and then cover with boiling water. Leave for 30 seconds, then plunge into cold water and peel the skin away from the cross. Scoop out tomato seeds with a teaspoon, chop the flesh and place in a large baking dish.

Stir in leek, garlic, fennel, olive oil, Pernod, bay leaves and thyme. Mix well and then set aside for at least 30 minutes, or preferably several hours if possible, to allow flavours to fully develop.

Cover the dish and bake for about 30 minutes. Add the potato, beans, stock and wine, mix well, then cover and bake for 35–45 minutes, or until potato is cooked through. Remove the bay leaves and thyme sprigs.

Serve in warmed bowls, topped with a spoonful of pesto.

Serves 4–6

Channa masala

1 cup (220 g/7 oz) dried chickpeas
2 tablespoons oil
2 onions, finely chopped
2 large ripe tomatoes, chopped
½ teaspoon ground coriander
  (cilantro)
1 teaspoon ground cumin
1 teaspoon chilli powder
¼ teaspoon ground turmeric
1 tablespoon channa (chole) masala
  (see Note)
20 g (³/₄ oz) ghee or butter
1 small white onion, sliced
fresh mint and coriander (cilantro)
  leaves, to garnish

Place the chickpeas in a bowl, cover with water and to soak overnight.

Drain, rinse and place in a saucepan. Cover with plenty of water and bring to the boil, then reduce the heat and simmer for 40 minutes, or until the chickpeas are soft. Drain.

Heat oil in a large saucepan, add the onion and cook over medium heat for 15 minutes, or until golden brown. Add chopped tomato, cumin, ground coriander, chilli powder, the channa (chole) masala, turmeric, and 500 ml (16 fl oz/2 cups) cold water, and cook for 10 minutes. Add the chickpeas, season well with salt, then cook for 7–10 minutes, or until sauce thickens.

Transfer to a serving dish. Place the ghee or the butter on top and allow to melt before serving. Garnish with the sliced onion, mint and coriander.

Serves 6

Note: Channa (chole) masala is a spice blend specifically used in this dish. It is available at Indian grocery stores. Garam masala can be used as a substitute.

Meat soups

Chicken soup with couscous

1.5 kg (3 lb 5 oz) chicken, quartered
2 tablespoons olive oil
2 onions, finely chopped
½ teaspoon ground cumin
½ teaspoon paprika
½ teaspoon harissa, or to taste (or
   ¼ teaspoon cayenne pepper)
2 tomatoes
1 tablespoon tomato paste
   (concentrated purée)
1 teaspoon sugar
1 cinnamon stick
100 g (3½ oz/½ cup) couscous
2 tablespoons finely chopped flat-leaf
   (Italian) parsley
1 tablespoon finely chopped
   coriander (cilantro) leaves
1 teaspoon dried mint
lemon wedges, to serve

Remove and discard the skin from the chicken. Heat the olive oil in a large saucepan or stockpot, add the chicken and cook over high heat for 2–3 minutes, stirring often. Reduce the heat to medium, add onion and cook for 5 minutes, or until the onion has softened. Stir in cumin, paprika and harissa or cayenne pepper. Add 1 litre (35 fl oz/4 cups) water and bring to the boil.

Halve the tomatoes and squeeze out the seeds. Grate the tomatoes over a plate down to the skin, discarding the skin. Add grated tomato to the pot, along with the tomato paste, sugar, cinnamon stick, 1 teaspoon salt and some pepper. Bring to the boil, then reduce the heat to low, cover and simmer for 1 hour.

Remove the chicken to a dish using a slotted spoon. Remove the bones and tear the chicken meat into strips. Return the chicken to the pot with an additional 500 ml (17 fl oz/2 cups) water and return to the boil. While it is boiling, pour in couscous, stirring. Reduce heat, then stir in the parsley, coriander and the mint and simmer, uncovered, for 20 minutes. Adjust the seasoning and serve with lemon wedges and crusty bread.

Serves 4

Pork and chickpea stew

2 teaspoons ground cumin
1 teaspoon ground coriander
1/2 teaspoon chilli powder
1/4 teaspoon ground cinnamon
400 g (14 oz) lean diced pork,
    trimmed
1 tablespoon plain (all-purpose) flour
1 tablespoon olive oil
1 large onion, finely chopped
3 garlic cloves, finely chopped
2 large unpeeled carrots, chopped
2 celery stalks, sliced
250 ml (9 fl oz/1 cup) chicken stock
2 ripe tomatoes, chopped
310 g (11 oz) tinned chickpeas,
    drained and rinsed
2 tablespoons chopped parsley

Cook the spices in a dry frying pan over low heat, shaking the pan, for 1 minute, or until fragrant.

Combine the trimmed pork with the spices and flour in a plastic bag and toss well to coat. Remove pork from bag and shake off the excess flour.

Heat the oil in a large heavy-based saucepan over high heat and cook the pork, tossing regularly, for about 8 minutes, or until lightly browned. Add onion, garlic, carrot, celery and half the stock to the pan and toss well. Cover and cook for 10 minutes.

Add remaining stock and tomato and season with salt and freshly ground black pepper. Bring to the boil, then reduce heat and cover with a tight-fitting lid and simmer over low heat for 1 hour. Gently shake the pan occasionally but don't remove the lid during cooking. Stir in the chickpeas and parsley. Simmer, uncovered, for a further 5 minutes and serve.

Serves 4

Harira (chickpea, lamb and coriander soup)

2 tablespoons olive oil
2 small onions, chopped
2 large garlic cloves, crushed
500 g (1 lb 2 oz) lamb shoulder
  steaks, trimmed of excess fat and
  sinew, cut into small chunks
1 1/2 teaspoons ground cumin
2 teaspoons paprika
1/2 teaspoon ground cloves
1 bay leaf
2 tablespoons tomato paste (purée)
1 litre (35 fl oz/4 cups) beef stock
900 g (2 lb) tinned chickpeas, rinsed
  and drained
800 g (1 lb 10 oz) tinned chopped
  tomatoes
30 g (1 oz) finely chopped coriander
  (cilantro)
coriander (cilantro) leaves and small
  black olives, to garnish
toasted pitta bread, to serve

Heat the oil in a large, heavy-based saucepan or stockpot, add onion and garlic and cook for 5 minutes, or until softened. Add the meat, in batches, and cook over a high heat until browned all over. Return all the meat to the pan.

Add spices and bay leaf to the pan and cook until fragrant. Add tomato paste and cook for about 2 minutes, stirring constantly. Add the stock to the pan, stir well and bring to the boil.

Add chickpeas, tomato and chopped coriander to the pan. Stir, then bring to the boil. Reduce heat and simmer, covered, for about 2 hours, or until the meat is tender. Stir occasionally. Season with salt and pepper, to taste.

Garnish with the coriander leaves and small black olives. Serve with toasted pitta bread drizzled with a little extra virgin olive oil.

Serves 4–6

Chestnut, pancetta and cabbage soup

100 g (3½ oz) cavolo nero or savoy
 cabbage, roughly chopped
2 tablespoons olive oil
1 large onion, finely chopped
200 g (7 oz) pancetta, diced
3 garlic cloves, crushed
10 g (¼ oz) rosemary, chopped
300 g (10½ oz) cooked peeled
 chestnuts
170 ml (5½ fl oz/⅔ cup) red wine
drizzle of extra virgin olive oil

Cook the cabbage in 1.5 litres
(52 fl oz/6 cups) boiling salted water
for about 10 minutes. Drain, reserving
the water. Rinse the cabbage in cold
water if too hot to handle, and chop
more finely.

Heat the olive oil in a large saucepan
and cook the onion and pancetta over
moderately high heat until the onion is
soft and the pancetta lightly browned.
Add the garlic and rosemary and cook
for a few minutes. Break up chestnuts
a little and then add to the pan with
the cabbage. Stir to infuse flavours,
season, then add wine. Bring to the
boil and cook for a couple of minutes.
Add the cabbage water and simmer
for 15 minutes.

Purée half of the soup, leaving the
remainder unpuréed to create a little
texture. Serve hot with a drizzle of
extra virgin olive oil over each bowl.

Serves 4

Avgolemono soup with chicken

1 onion, halved
2 cloves
1 carrot, cut into chunks
1 bay leaf
500 g (1 lb 2 oz) chicken breast fillets
75 g (2½ oz/⅓ cup) short-grain rice
3 eggs, separated
3 tablespoons lemon juice
2 tablespoons chopped flat-leaf
   (Italian) parsley
4 thin lemon slices, to garnish

Stud onion with cloves and place in a large saucepan with 1.5 litres (52 fl oz/6 cups) water. Add carrot, the bay leaf and chicken and season. Slowly bring to the boil, then reduce the heat and simmer for 10 minutes, or until the chicken is cooked.

Strain stock into a clean saucepan, reserving the chicken and discarding the vegetables. Add rice to the stock, bring to the boil, then reduce the heat and simmer for 15 minutes, or until the rice is tender. Shred the chicken.

Whisk the egg whites in a clean dry bowl until stiff peaks form, then beat in the yolks. Slowly beat in the lemon juice. Gently stir in about 150 ml (5 fl oz) of the hot (not boiling) stock and beat thoroughly. Add the egg mixture to the stock and heat gently, but do not let it boil otherwise the eggs may scramble. Add the chicken and season.

Set aside for 2–3 minutes to allow the flavours to develop, then sprinkle the parsley over the top. Garnish with the lemon slices.

Serves 4

Rice soup with prawns and chicken

110 g (4 oz) raw prawns (shrimp)
2 tablespoons vegetable oil
3–4 large garlic cloves, finely chopped
1 coriander (cilantro) root, finely chopped
1 garlic clove, extra, roughly chopped
a pinch of ground white pepper, plus extra, to sprinkle
75 g (3 oz) minced (ground) chicken or pork
1 spring onion (scallion), finely chopped
935 ml (31 fl oz/3¾ cups) chicken or vegetable stock
2 tablespoons light soy sauce
2 teaspoons preserved radish
325 g (11½ oz/1¾ cups) cooked jasmine rice
1 tablespoon finely sliced ginger
1 Chinese cabbage leaf, roughly chopped
2 spring onions (scallions), finely chopped, for garnish
a few coriander (cilantro) leaves, for garnish

Peel and devein prawns and cut each prawn along the back so it opens like a butterfly (leave each prawn joined along the base and at the tail, leaving the tail attached).

Heat oil in a small wok or frying pan and stir-fry the finely chopped garlic until light golden. Remove from the heat and discard the garlic.

Using a pestle and mortar or a small blender, pound or blend the coriander root, roughly chopped garlic, pepper and a pinch of salt into a paste. In a bowl, combine the coriander paste with the chicken or pork and spring onion. Shape the mixture into small balls about 1 cm (½ inch) across.

Heat the stock to boiling point in a saucepan. Add thelight soy sauce, preserved radish and rice. Lower the meatballs into the stock over a medium heat and cook for 3 minutes or until the chicken is cooked. Add prawns, ginger and Chinese cabbage to stock. Cook for 1–2 minutes or until the prawns open and turn pink.

Garnish with the spring onions and the coriander leaves. Sprinkle with ground white pepper and garlic oil.

Serves 4

Moroccan chickpea, lamb and coriander soup

165 g (5³/₄ oz/³/₄ cup) dried
  chickpeas
1 tablespoon olive oil
850 g (1 lb 14 oz) boned lamb leg,
  cut into 1 cm (¹/₂ in) cubes
1 onion, chopped
2 garlic cloves, crushed
¹/₂ teaspoon ground cinnamon
¹/₂ teaspoon ground turmeric
¹/₂ teaspoon ground ginger
4 tablespoons chopped coriander
  (cilantro) leaves
800 g (1 lb 12 oz) tinned diced
  tomatoes
1 litre (35 fl oz/4 cups) chicken stock
135 g (4³/₄ oz/²/₃ cup) red lentils
fresh coriander (cilantro) leaves,
  to garnish
Turkish bread, to serve

Put the chickpeas in a large bowl, cover with water and soak overnight. Drain and rinse under cold water and drain again.

Heat the oil in a large saucepan over high heat. Add the lamb and brown in batches for 2–3 minutes. Reduce the heat to medium, return all the lamb to the pan along with onion and garlic and cook for 5 minutes. Add tumeric, cinnamon, ginger, a pinch of salt and 1 teaspoon freshly ground black pepper and then cook for a further 2 minutes. Add chopped coriander, tomatoes, stock and about 500 ml (17 fl oz/2 cups) water and bring to the boil over high heat.

Rinse lentils under cold water and drain. Add lentils and chickpeas to the pan, then reduce the heat and simmer, covered, for 1¹/₂ hours. Uncover and cook for a further 30 minutes, or until lamb is tender and soup is thick. Season to taste. Divide soup among serving bowls and garnish with the coriander. Serve with toasted Turkish bread.

Serves 4–6

Borlotti bean and Italian sausage soup

2 tablespoons olive oil
3 thin Italian sausages
100 g (3½ oz) thickly sliced pancetta,
  cut into 5 mm x 2 cm
  (¼ inch x ¾ inch) strips
2 onions, chopped
1 leek, white part only, sliced
2 garlic cloves, chopped
2 celery stalks, chopped
2 carrots, chopped
2 large thyme sprigs
1 litre (35 fl oz/4 cups) chicken stock
  or vegetable stock
400 g (14 oz) tinned borlotti
  (cranberry) beans, rinsed and
  drained
410 g (14½ oz) tinned diced
  tomatoes
2 large handfuls flat-leaf (Italian)
  parsley, chopped

Heat a little of the oil in a large frying pan over medium heat. Fry the sausages for 5–6 minutes, or until browned all over. Add the pancetta halfway through cooking. Remove from the heat and set aside.

Heat the remaining oil in a large heavy-based saucepan and add the onion, leek, garlic, celery and carrot. Stir for 2 minutes to coat the vegetables in the oil. Reduce the heat, cover and simmer, stirring occasionally, for 10 minutes. Do not allow the vegetables to brown.

Add the thyme sprigs and stock. Slowly bring to the boil, then reduce the heat and simmer, covered, for 20 minutes. Add the beans and remove the thyme sprigs. Remove the saucepan from the heat.

Using an immersion blender fitted with the chopping blade, whizz for 30 seconds, or until the soup is puréed but still has some texture.

Dice the sausages and add them to the soup along with the pancetta and diced tomatoes. Gently reheat the soup. Stir through the parsley and season with plenty of salt and freshly ground black pepper.

Serves 4

Chicken noodle soup

3 dried Chinese mushrooms
185 g (6½ oz) dried thin egg noodles
1 tablespoon oil
4 spring onions (scallions), cut into
    fine shreds
1 tablespoon soy sauce
2 tablespoons rice wine, mirin or
    sherry
1.25 litres (44 fl oz/5 cups) chicken
    stock
½ small barbecued chicken,
    shredded
60 g (2¼ oz) sliced ham, cut into
    strips
90 g (3¼ oz) bean sprouts
coriander (cilantro) leaves and thinly
    sliced red chilli, to garnish

Soak the mushrooms in boiling water for 10 minutes to soften them. Squeeze dry, then remove the tough stems from the mushrooms and slice the caps thinly.

Cook the noodles in a large pan of boiling water for 3 minutes, or according to the packet directions. Drain and cut the noodles into shorter lengths with scissors.

Heat the oil in a large heavy-based saucepan. Add the mushrooms and spring onion. Cook for 1 minute, then add the soy sauce, rice wine and stock. Bring slowly to the boil and cook for 1 minute. Reduce the heat then add the noodles, shredded chicken, ham and bean sprouts. Heat through for 2 minutes without allowing to boil.

Use tongs to divide the noodles among four bowls, ladle in the remaining mixture, and garnish with coriander leaves and sliced chilli.

Serves 4

Note: Rice wine and mirin are available at Asian food stores.

Eight-treasure noodle soup

10 g (¼ oz) dried shiitake mushrooms
375 g (12 oz) fresh thick egg noodles
1.25 litres (44 fl oz/5 cups) chicken
  stock
60 ml (2 fl oz/¼ cup) light soy sauce
2 teaspoons Chinese rice wine
200 g (7 oz) chicken breast fillet, cut
  into 1 cm (½ in) strips on the
  diagonal
200 g (7 oz) Chinese barbecued pork
  (char sui), cut into 5 mm (¼ in)
  slices
¼ onion, finely chopped
1 carrot, cut into 1 cm (½ in) slices on
  the diagonal
120 g (4¼ oz) snow peas, cut in half
  on the diagonal
4 spring onions (scallions), thinly
  sliced

Soak the mushrooms in boiling water for 20 minutes, or until soft. Drain and squeeze out any excess liquid. Discard the stems and thinly slice the caps.

Bring a large saucepan of water to the boil and cook the noodles for 1 minute, or until they are cooked through. Drain, then rinse with cold water. Divide evenly among four deep warmed serving bowls.

Meanwhile, bring the chicken stock to the boil in a large saucepan over high heat. Reduce heat to medium and stir in the soy sauce and the rice wine. Simmer for 2 minutes. Add the chicken and pork and then cook for 2 minutes, or until chicken is cooked and the pork is heated through. Add onion, carrot, snow peas, mushrooms and half the spring onion, and cook for 1 minute, or until carrot is tender.

Divide vegetables and meat among the serving bowls and ladle on the hot broth. Garnish with the rest of the spring onion.

Serves 4

Baby corn and chicken soup

150 g (5½ oz) whole baby corn
1 tablespoon oil
2 lemongrass stems, white part only, very thinly sliced
2 tablespoons grated fresh ginger
6 spring onions (scallions), chopped
1 red chilli, finely chopped
1 litre (35 fl oz/4 cups) chicken stock
375 ml (13 fl oz/1½ cups) coconut milk
250 g (9 oz) boneless, skinless chicken breasts, thinly sliced
135 g (4¾ oz) creamed corn
1 tablespoon soy sauce
2 tablespoons finely snipped chives, to serve
1 red chilli, thinly sliced, to serve

Cut the baby corn in half or quarters lengthways, depending on their size.

Heat oil in a saucepan over medium heat and cook lemongrass, ginger, spring onion and chilli for 1 minute, stirring continuously. Add the stock and coconut milk and bring to the boil—do not cover or the coconut milk will curdle.

Add corn, chicken and creamed corn and simmer for 8 minutes, or until the corn and chicken are just tender. Add the soy sauce, season well and serve garnished with the chives and chilli.

Serves 4

Vegetable soup with chicken and prawn

175 g (6 oz) raw prawns (shrimp)
2 coriander (cilantro) roots, cleaned
  and finely chopped
2 garlic cloves, roughly chopped
pinch of ground white pepper, plus
  extra, to sprinkle
150 g (5½ oz) minced (ground)
  chicken
½ spring onion (scallion), finely
  chopped
935 ml (3¾ cups) chicken or
  vegetable stock
2 tablespoons light soy sauce
2 teaspoons preserved radish
175 g (6 oz) marrow or pumpkin
  (squash), cut into 2.5 cm (1 in)
  cubes
175 g (6 oz) Chinese cabbage,
  roughly chopped
a few coriander (cilantro) leaves, for
  garnish

Peel and devein the prawns and cut each prawn along the back so it opens like a butterfly (leave each prawn joined along the base and at the tail, leaving the tail attached).

Using a pestle and mortar or a small blender, pound or blend coriander roots, garlic, pepper and a pinch of salt into a paste. In a bowl, combine the coriander paste with the chicken and spring onion. Use a spoon or your wet hands to shape the chicken mixture into small balls about 1 cm (½ in) across.

Heat the stock to boiling point in a saucepan. Add the light soy sauce and preserved radish. Lower chicken balls into the stock and cook over a medium heat for 1–2 minutes or until the balls are cooked.

Add marrow to pan and cook for 2–3 minutes. Add the prawns and Chinese cabbage and then cook for another 1–2 minutes. Taste, then adjust seasoning if necessary. Garnish with the coriander leaves. Sprinkle with ground white pepper.

Serves 4

Thai-style chicken and corn soup

425 g (15 oz) tinned corn kernels, undrained
2 chicken stock (bouillon) cubes, crumbled
8 spring onions (scallions), sliced
1 tablespoon finely chopped fresh ginger
500 g (1 lb 2 oz) skinless chicken breast, trimmed and thinly sliced
1 tablespoon sweet chilli sauce
1 tablespoon fish sauce
200 g (7 oz) fresh thin rice noodles
2 large handfuls coriander (cilantro) leaves, chopped
2 teaspoons grated lime zest
2 tablespoons lime juice

Bring 1 litre (35 fl oz/4 cups) water to the boil in a large saucepan over high heat. Add the corn kernels and their juice, the stock cubes, spring onion and ginger, then reduce the heat and simmer for 1 minute.

Add chicken, sweet chilli sauce and fish sauce and simmer for 3 minutes, or until chicken is cooked through.

Put the noodles in a large heatproof bowl, cover with boiling water and soak for 5 minutes, or until softened. Separate gently and drain.

Add the noodles, coriander, lime zest and lime juice to the soup and serve immediately.

Serves 4

Chicken, coconut and galangal soup

750 ml (26 fl oz/3 cups) coconut milk
2 lemon grass stalks, white part only,
    each cut into a tassel or bruised
5 cm (2 inch) piece of galangal,
    cut into several pieces
4 Asian shallots, smashed with the flat
    side of a cleaver
400 g (14 oz) skinless chicken breast
    fillets, cut into slices
2 tablespoons fish sauce
1 tablespoon palm sugar
200 g (7 oz) baby tomatoes, cut into
    bite-sized pieces if large
150 g (5½ oz) straw mushrooms or
    button mushrooms
3 tablespoons lime juice
6 kaffir lime leaves, torn in half
3–5 bird's eye chillies, stems
    removed, bruised, or 2 long red
    chillies, seeded and finely sliced a
    few coriander (cilantro) leaves, to
    garnish

Put the coconut milk, lemongrass, galangal and shallots in a saucepan or wok over a medium heat and bring to a boil.

Add chicken, fish sauce and palm sugar and simmer, stirring constantly for 5 minutes or until the chicken is cooked through.

Add tomatoes and mushrooms and simmer for 2–3 minutes. Add lime juice, makrut lime leaves and chillies in the last few seconds, taking care not to let tomatoes lose their shape. Taste, then adjust the seasoning if necessary. This dish is not meant to be overwhelmingly hot, but to have a sweet, salty, sour taste. Serve garnished with coriander leaves.

Serves 4

Portuguese chicken broth with rice

2.5 litres (85 fl oz/10 cups) chicken
  stock
1 onion, cut into thin wedges
1 teaspoon grated lemon zest
1 fresh mint sprig
500 g (1 lb 2 oz) potatoes, chopped
1 tablespoon olive oil
2 chicken breast fillets
200 g (7 oz/1 cup) long-grain rice
2 tablespoons lemon juice
shredded mint, to garnish

Combine chicken stock, onion, lemon zest, mint sprig, potato and olive oil in a large saucepan. Slowly bring to the boil, then reduce the heat, add the chicken breasts and simmer gently for 20–25 minutes, or until the chicken is cooked through.

Remove the chicken breasts and discard the mint sprig. Cool the chicken, then cut it into thin slices.

Meanwhile, add the rice to the pan and simmer for 25–30 minutes, or until the rice is tender. Return sliced chicken to the pan, add lemon juice and stir for 1–2 minutes, or until the chicken is warmed through. Season, and serve garnished with mint.

Serves 6

Note: Rice and potato absorb liquid on standing, so serve immediately.

Hot beef borscht

500 g (1 lb 2 oz) gravy beef, cut into
  large pieces
500 g (1 lb 2 oz) fresh beetroot
1 onion, finely chopped
1 carrot, cut into short strips
1 parsnip, cut into short strips
75 g (2½ oz/1 cup) finely shredded
  cabbage
sour cream and chopped chives,
  to serve

Put beef and 1 litre (35 fl oz/4 cups)
water in a heavy-based saucepan,
and bring slowly to the boil. Reduce
heat, cover and simmer for 1 hour.
Skim the surface as required.

Cut the stems from beetroot, wash
well and place in a large, heavy-based
saucepan with 1 litre (35 fl oz/4 cups)
water. Bring to the boil, reduce the
heat and simmer for 40 minutes, or
until tender. Drain, reserving 250 ml
(9 fl oz/1 cup) of the liquid. Cool, then
peel and grate the beetroot.

Remove meat from the stock, cool
and dice. Return the meat to stock
and add the onion, carrot, parsnip,
beetroot and reserved liquid. Bring
to the boil, reduce the heat, cover
and simmer for 45 minutes.

Stir in the cabbage and simmer for a
further 15 minutes. Season to taste.
Serve with the sour cream and chives.

Serves 4–6

Cauliflower, cannellini bean and prosciutto soup

2 tablespoons olive oil
100 g (3½ oz/about 8 slices)
  prosciutto, chopped
1 onion, chopped
1 garlic clove, minced
800 g (1 lb 12 oz) cauliflower, cut into
  small florets
800 g (1 lb 12 oz) tinned cannellini
  beans, drained
125 ml (4 fl oz/½ cup) thick cream
snipped chives, to serve

Heat 1 tablespoon of oil in a large saucepan over medium–high heat. Add the prosciutto and fry, stirring often, until crisp. Transfer half of the prosciutto to a plate lined with paper towel and leave remaining prosciutto in the saucepan.

Reduce the heat to medium. Add the remaining oil and the onion to the saucepan and fry for 5 minutes, or until softened. Add the garlic and cauliflower florets and fry for 3 minutes.

Add the cannellini beans and 1 litre (35 fl oz/4 cups) of water and season well with salt and freshly ground black pepper. Bring to the boil, then reduce the heat and simmer, covered, for 15 minutes, or until the cauliflower is tender. Set aside to cool for about 10 minutes.

Using an immersion blender fitted with chopping blade, whizz soup for 25 seconds, or until smooth. Season with salt and freshly ground black pepper. Stir through cream and gently reheat soup. Serve immediately, with reserved crisp prosciutto and chives sprinkled on top.

Serves 4

Vietnamese pork and prawn ball soup with cellophane noodles

Pork and prawn balls
2 garlic cloves, roughly chopped
1 lemongrass stem, white part only,
  sliced
300 g (10½ oz) pork spareribs, skin
  and bones removed, cut into
  chunks
125 g (4½ oz) raw king prawns
  (shrimp), peeled and deveined
1 small handful coriander (cilantro)
  leaves
2 teaspoons fish sauce

1.5 litres (52 fl oz/6 cups) chicken
  stock
1 lemongrass stem, white part only,
  sliced
1 small red chilli, sliced
8 raw prawns (shrimp), peeled and
  deveined, leaving the tails intact
100 g (3½ oz) bean vermicelli noodles
  (cellophane noodles)
1–2 teaspoons fish sauce, to taste
60 ml (2 fl oz/¼ cup) lime juice
90 g (3¼ oz/1 cup) bean sprouts,
  trimmed
1 handful Vietnamese mint, to serve
1 handful coriander (cilantro) leaves,
  to serve

To make the pork and prawn balls, put garlic, lemon grass and pork in a small processor fitted with the metal blade and whizz for 20–35 seconds, or until finely chopped, occasionally scraping down the side of processor bowl. Add the prawns, coriander and fish sauce and whizz in short bursts until the prawns are chopped but still large enough to give the balls some texture. Roll 2 teaspoons of mixture at a time into small balls.

Heat the stock in a saucepan, add the lemongrass and chilli and bring to the boil. Add pork and prawn balls and simmer for 5 minutes. Add prawns and noodles and simmer over low heat for 1–2 minutes, or until prawns have a tinge of orange and are almost cooked. Add the fish sauce, to taste, and lime juice.

Ladle the soup into four bowls and serve the bean sprouts, Vietnamese mint and coriander on top.

Serves 4

Note: Use pork spareribs with good layers of meat and fat.

Galician-style soup

250 g (9 oz/1¼ cups) dried white
    haricot beans (such as navy beans)
500 g (1 lb 2 oz) smoked ham hock
2 tablespoons olive oil
1 leek, chopped
1 garlic clove, chopped
500 g (1 lb 2 oz) pork baby back or
    American-style ribs, separated into
    5 cm (2 in) widths
2 all-purpose potatoes, peeled and
    cubed
1 bay leaf
1 kg (2 lb 4 oz) silverbeet (Swiss
    chard), washed well and chopped

Rinse the beans, then soak them in cold water for at least 5 hours. Put the ham hock in a large heavy-based saucepan and cover with cold water. Bring to the boil, then reduce the heat and simmer for about 1 hour, or until the meat starts to come away from the bone. Remove from heat. Remove the meat from the bone and cut into 2 cm (³/₄ in) cubes. Reserve 625 ml (21½ fl oz/2½ cups) of the liquid.

Meanwhile, put the beans in a large saucepan and cover with cold water. Bring to the boil, then reduce the heat and simmer for 30 minutes. Drain, reserving 250 ml (9 fl oz/1 cup) of the cooking liquid.

Heat the olive oil in a large heavy-based saucepan over medium heat and cook the leek and garlic for about 5 minutes, or until translucent. Add the ham, beans, pork or ribs, potato, bay leaf and reserved cooking liquid.

Bring to the boil, then reduce the heat, cover and simmer for about 45 minutes. Stir in the silverbeet and cook for a further 5 minutes. Season before serving.

Serves 4

Spicy lamb soup

2 large onions, roughly chopped
3 red chillies, seeded and chopped
  (or 2 teaspoons dried chilli)
3–4 garlic cloves
2.5 cm (1 in) piece fresh ginger,
  peeled and chopped
5 cm (2 in) lemongrass, white part
  only, finely chopped
1/2 teaspoon ground cardamom
2 teaspoons ground cumin
1/2 teaspoon ground cinnamon
1 teaspoon ground turmeric
2 tablespoons peanut oil
1.5 kg (3 lb 5 oz) lamb neck chops
2–3 tablespoons vindaloo paste
600 ml (21 fl oz) coconut cream
3 tablespoons soft brown sugar
2–3 tablespoons lime juice
4 kaffir lime leaves

Put onion, chilli, garlic, ginger, cumin, lemongrass, cardamom, cinnamon, tumeric and 1 teaspoon ground black pepper in a food processor and then process to a paste. Heat half the oil in a large frying pan and brown chops in batches. Drain on paper towels.

Add the remaining oil to the pan and cook the spice and vindaloo pastes for 2–3 minutes. Add the chops and 1.75 litres (61 fl oz/7 cups) water, cover and bring to the boil. Reduce the heat and simmer, covered, for 1 hour. Remove chops from the pan and stir in coconut cream. Remove the meat from the bones, shred and return to the pan.

Add the sugar, lime juice and makrut leaves. Simmer, uncovered, over low heat for 20–25 minutes, until slightly thickened.

Serves 4–6

Mulligatawny soup

30 g (1 oz) butter
375 g (13 oz) chicken thigh cutlets,
  skin and fat removed
1 large onion, finely chopped
1 apple, peeled, cored and diced
1 tablespoon curry paste
2 tablespoons plain (all-purpose) flour
750 ml (26 fl oz/3 cups) chicken stock
3 tablespoons basmati rice
1 tablespoon chutney
1 tablespoon lemon juice
3 tablespoons cream

Heat butter in a large heavy-based saucepan and brown the chicken for 5 minutes, then remove from the pan. Add the onion, apple and curry paste to the pan. Cook for 5 minutes, or until the onion is soft. Stir in the flour, cook for 2 minutes then add half the stock. Stir until the mixture boils and thickens.

Return the chicken to the pan with the remaining stock. Stir until boiling, reduce the heat, cover and simmer for 45 minutes. Add the rice and cook for a further 15 minutes.

Remove the chicken, dice the meat finely and return to the pan. Add the chutney, lemon juice, cream and salt and pepper to taste.

Serves 4

Vietnamese beef soup

400 g (14 oz) lean rump steak,
  trimmed
1/2 onion
1 1/2 tbs fish sauce
1 star anise
1 cinnamon stick
pinch ground white pepper
1.5 litres (52 fl oz/6 cups) beef stock
300 g (10 1/2 oz) fresh thin rice noodles
3 spring onions (scallions), thinly
  sliced
1 small handful Vietnamese mint
  leaves
90 g (3 1/4 oz/1 cup) bean sprouts,
  trimmed
1 small onion, halved and thinly sliced
1 small red chilli, thinly sliced on the
  diagonal
lemon wedges, to serve

Wrap the steak in plastic wrap and freeze it for 40 minutes as this will make it easier to slice.

Meanwhile, put the onion half, fish sauce, star anise, cinnamon stick, white pepper, stock and 500 ml (17 fl oz/2 cups) water in a large saucepan. Bring to the boil, then reduce heat, cover and simmer for 20 minutes. Discard the onion, star anise and cinnamon stick.

Put noodles in a large heatproof bowl. Cover with boiling water and soak for 5 minutes, or until softened. Seperate gently and drain. Thinly slice the meat across the grain.

Divide the noodles and spring onion among four deep bowls. Top with beef, mint, bean sprouts, thinly sliced onion and chilli. Ladle hot broth over the top and serve with the lemon wedges—the heat of liquid will cook the beef.

Serves 4

Chicken consomme

Stock
1 kg (2 lb 4 oz) chicken carcasses,
　halved
185 g (6½ oz) chicken legs
1 carrot, chopped
1 onion, chopped
1 celery stalk, chopped
2 parsley sprigs
20 black peppercorns
1 bay leaf
1 thyme sprig

Clarification mixture
2 chicken drumsticks
1 carrot, finely chopped
1 leek, finely chopped
1 celery stalk, finely chopped
10 black peppercorns
1 parsley sprig, chopped
2 tomatoes, chopped
2 egg whites, lightly beaten

1 small carrot, julienned
½ small leek, white part only,
　julienned

To make stock, remove any skin and fat from chicken carcasses and legs and place in a large heavy-based saucepan along with with 3 litres (102 fl oz/12 cups) cold water. Bring to the boil. Add remaining ingredients and simmer for 1½ hours, skimming occasionally. Strain stock and return to the saucepan.

To make clarification mixture, remove the skin and meat from drumsticks and discard the skin. Chop the meat finely and mix with the carrot, leek, celery, peppercorns, parsley, tomato and egg white. Add 190 ml (6½ fl oz) of the warm stock.

Add the clarification mixture to the strained stock and whisk in well. Bring to a gentle simmer. Simmer for 1 hour.

Ladle out chicken stock and strain through a fine sieve lined with damp muslin. Place sheets of paper towel over the top and quickly lift away to remove any remaining fat. Season.

Just before serving, reheat the soup. Place the julienned vegetables in a saucepan of boiling water and cook for 2 minutes. Drain, then spoon into bowls and pour soup over the top.

Serves 4

Lamb and chickpea soup

500 g (1 lb 2 oz) boneless lamb
  shoulder
2 tablespoons olive oil
2 small brown onions, chopped
2 large garlic cloves, crushed
1½ teaspoons ground cumin
2 teaspoons paprika
1 bay leaf
2 tablespoons tomato paste
  (concentrated purée)
1 litre (35 fl oz/4 cups) beef stock
600 g (1 lb 5 oz) tinned chickpeas
800 g (1 lb 12 oz) tinned chopped
  tomatoes
3 tablespoons finely chopped
  coriander (cilantro) leaves
3 tablespoons finely chopped flat-leaf
  (Italian) parsley
coriander (cilantro) leaves, extra,
  to serve

Trim lamb of excess fat and sinew.
Cut the lamb into small chunks.

Heat olive oil in a large heavy-based
saucepan or stockpot, add the onion
and garlic and cook over low heat for
5 minutes, or until onion is soft. Add
the meat, increase heat to medium
and stir until meat changes colour.

Add cumin, paprika and bay leaf to
the pan and cook until fragrant. Add
the tomato paste and cook for about
2 minutes, stirring constantly. Add
beef stock to the pan, stir well and
bring to the boil.

Drain the chickpeas, rinse them
and add to the pan, along with the
tomatoes and chopped coriander
and parsley. Stir, then bring to the
boil. Reduce heat and simmer for
2 hours, or until the meat is tender.
Stir occasionally. Season, to taste.
Garnish with the extra coriander.

Serves 4

Ham and pea soup

2 tablespoons olive oil
1 large onion, chopped
3 celery stalks, sliced
about 40 sage leaves
220 g (7³/₄ oz/1 cup) green split peas,
　rinsed and drained
1 smoked ham hock, about 800 g
　(1 lb 12 oz)
1 thyme sprig
vegetable oil, for pan-frying

Heat the oil in a large saucepan over medium heat. Add onion, celery and four of the sage leaves and fry, stirring often, for 5 minutes, or until the onion and celery are soft.

Add the green split peas, ham hock, thyme sprig and 1.25 litres (44 fl oz/ 5 cups) of water. Bring to the boil, then reduce heat, cover and simmer for 1½ hours, or until meat is falling off the bone.

Remove saucepan from the heat and discard the thyme sprig. Remove the ham hock from the saucepan and, when cool enough to handle, cut off meat and return it to soup. Discard the bone. Using an immersion blender fitted with the chopping blade, whizz soup for 30 seconds, or until smooth. Season with salt and pepper..

Pour vegetable oil into a saucepan to a depth of 3 cm (1¼ in) and heat over high heat. Add remaining sage leaves and fry for a few seconds, or until they turn bright green and become crisp. Remove using a slotted spoon and drain.

Reheat the soup and ladle into four bowls. Sprinkle the sage leaves on top. Serve with crispbread.

Serves 4

Creamy chicken and paprika soup

90 g (3¼ oz) butter
1 onion, finely chopped
1 celery stalk, finely chopped
1 small carrot, finely chopped
2 tablespoons Hungarian sweet
  paprika
40 g (1½ oz/⅓ cup) plain
  (all-purpose) flour
2 litres (70 fl oz/8 cups) chicken stock
125 ml (4 fl oz/½ cup) cream
300 g (10½ oz) boneless, skinless
  cooked chicken breasts, finely
  chopped
crusty bread, to serve

In a large saucepan, melt butter over medium–high heat. Add carrot onion and celery and cook for 5 minutes, or until vegetables have softened.

Add paprika and cook for 1 minute, or until the paprika becomes fragrant. Quickly toss in flour and stir until well combined. Cook for a further 1 minute and remove from the heat.

Add one-third of the stock and mix to a thick paste, stirring out all the lumps. Return pan to the heat and add the remaining stock. Stir until the soup boils and thickens slightly. Reduce the heat, cover and simmer for 45–50 minutes.

Remove the soup from the heat and stir in the cream and chicken. Season to taste and serve with crusty bread.

Serves 4–6

Meat
stews

Gypsy stew

250 g (9 oz/1¼ cups) dried white
 haricot beans (such as navy beans)
80 ml (2½ fl oz/⅓ cup) olive oil
2 garlic cloves, chopped
2 brown onions, chopped
1 teaspoon sweet paprika
 (pimentón)
1 teaspoon smoked paprika
 (pimentón)
2 teaspoons ground cumin
¼ teaspoon ground cinnamon
¼ teaspoon cayenne pepper
1 teaspoon dried rosemary
1 red capsicum (pepper), seeded and
 diced
750 g (1 lb 10 oz) pork tenderloin,
 roughly diced
400 g (14 oz) tinned chopped
 tomatoes
250 ml (9 fl oz/1 cup chicken stock)
300 g (10½ oz) orange sweet potato,
 peeled and roughly diced.
60 g (2¼ oz) silverbeet (Swiss chard),
 washed well and shredded.

Cover beans with water and soak for at least 3 hours. Drain well. Preheat the oven to 160°C (315°F/Gas 2-3). Heat 2 tablespoons of oil in a large saucepan over medium heat, add half the garlic and half the onion and cook for 5 minute, or until soft. Add beans and cover with water. Bring to the boil, then reduce the heat and simmer for 45 minutes, or until beans are soft.

Meanwhile, heat remaining oil in a large flameproof casserole dish over medium heat. Add remaining garlic and onion and cook for 5 minutes, or until softened. Stir in the spices, rosemary, capsicum and diced pork and cook until the pork is evenly pale brown. Add tomato and stock, bring to the boil, then cover and cook in oven for 1 hour. Add the beans and sweet potato, top up with 250 ml (9 fl oz/1 cup) water and return to the oven for 30 minutes, or until sweet potato is tender. Stir in the silverbeet and cook for 5 minutes, or until the silverbeet is wilted. Season to taste.

Serves 4

Chicken provençale

1 tablespoon olive oil
1.5 kg (3 lb 5 oz) chicken pieces
1 onion, chopped
1 red capsicum (pepper), chopped
4 tablespoons dry white wine
4 tablespoons chicken stock
425 g (15 oz) tinned chopped
  tomatoes
2 tablespoons tomato paste
  (concentrated purée)
90 g (3¼ oz/½ cup) black olives
small handful basil, shredded

Heat oil in a saucepan over high heat, add chicken, in batches, and cook for 3–4 minutes, or until it is browned. Return all chicken to the pan and add the onion and capsicum. Cook for 2–3 minutes, or until the onion is soft.

Add the wine, stock, tomato, tomato paste and olives and bring to the boil. Reduce the heat, cover and simmer for 30 minutes. Remove lid, turn the chicken pieces over and then cook for another 30 minutes, or until the chicken is tender and the sauce has thickened. Season to taste, sprinkle with the basil and serve with rice.

Serves 6

Osso buco alla Milanese

12 pieces veal shank,
plain (all-purpose) flour, seasoned
  with salt and pepper
60 ml (2 fl oz/¼ cup) olive oil
60 g (2¼ oz) butter
1 garlic clove
250 ml (9 fl oz/1 cup) dry white wine
1 bay leaf or lemon leaf
pinch of allspice
pinch of ground cinnamon

Gremolata
2 teaspoons grated lemon zest
6 tablespoons finely chopped parsley
1 garlic clove, finely chopped

lemon wedges, to serve

Tie each piece of veal shank around its girth to secure the flesh, then dust with the seasoned flour. Heat the oil, butter and garlic in a large, heavy saucepan big enough to hold shanks in a single layer. Put the shanks in the pan and cook for 12–15 minutes until well browned. Arrange the shanks, standing them up in a single layer, pour in wine and add bay leaf, allspice and cinnamon. Cover the saucepan.

Cook at a low simmer for 15 minutes, then add 125 ml (4 fl oz/½ cup) warm water. Continue cooking, with the lid of the saucepan on, for 45 minutes to 1 hour until meat is tender and can be cut with a fork. Check the volume of the liquid once or twice and add more water as needed. Transfer the veal to a plate and keep it warm. Discard the garlic clove and bay leaf.

To make the gremolata, mix together the lemon zest, parsley and the garlic. Increase the heat under the saucepan and stir for 1–2 minutes or until sauce is thick, scraping up any bits off the bottom of the saucepan as you stir. Stir in gremolata. Season if necessary and return the veal to the sauce. Heat through. Serve with lemon wedges.

Serves 4

Beef carbonnade

30 g (1 oz) butter
2–3 tablespoons oil
1 kg (2 lb 4 oz) lean beef rump or
  chuck steak, cubed
4 onions, chopped
1 garlic clove, crushed
1 teaspoon brown sugar
1 tablespoon plain (all-purpose) flour
500 ml (17 fl oz) beer (bitter or stout)
2 bay leaves
4 thyme sprigs

Croutons
6–8 slices baguette
dijon mustard

Preheat the oven to 150°C (300°F/
Gas 2). Melt the butter in a sauté pan
with a tablespoon of oil. Brown the
meat over high heat, then remove.

Add another tablespoon of oil to pan
and add onion. Cook over moderate
heat for 10 minutes, add the garlic
and sugar and then cook for a further
5 minutes, adding another tablespoon
of oil if necessary. Lift out the onion
onto a second plate.

Reduce the heat to low. Pour in any
juices that have drained from the
meat, then stir in flour. Remove from
the heat and stir in the beer. Return
to the heat and simmer.

Layer meat and onion in a casserole
dish, tucking the bay leaves and the
sprigs of thyme between the layers
and seasoning as you go. Pour the
liquid over the meat, cover with a lid
and cook in the oven for 2½–3 hours,
or until the meat is tender.

To make the croutons, preheat the
grill (broiler). Toast the baguette on
both sides, then spread one side
with mustard. Arrange on top of the
carbonnade, mustard side up, and
place the whole casserole under the
grill for 1 minute.

Serves 4

Mexican beef stew

500 g (1 lb 2 oz) roma (plum)
tomatoes, halved
6 flour tortillas
1–2 fresh red chillies, finely chopped
1 tablespoon olive oil
1 kg (2 lb 4 oz) stewing beef, cubed
1/2 teaspoon black pepper
2 onions, thinly sliced
375 ml (13 fl oz/1 1/2 cups) beef stock
60 g (2 1/4 oz/1/4 cup) tomato paste
375 g (13 oz) tinned kidney beans,
drained
1 teaspoon chilli powder
125 g (4 1/2 oz/1/2 cup) sour cream

Preheat the oven to 180°C (350°F/
Gas 4). Grill (broil) tomatoes, skin-side
up, under a hot grill for 6–8 minutes,
or until the skin is black and blistered.
Cool, remove the skin and roughly
chop the flesh.

Bake 2 of the tortillas for 4 minutes,
or until crisp. Break into pieces and
put in a food processor along with the
tomato and chilli. Process for about
30 seconds, or until almost smooth.

Heat the oil in a large heavy-based
saucepan. Brown beef in batches,
season with pepper, then remove.
Add onion to the pan and cook for
5 minutes. Return meat to the pan.
Stir in the processed mixture, stock
and tomato paste, and bring to the
boil. Reduce the heat, cover and
simmer for 1 1/4 hours. Add the beans
and chilli powder, and heat through.

Grill the remaining tortillas for about
2–3 minutes on each side, then cool
and cut into wedges. Serve the stew
with the sour cream, and toasted
tortilla wedges on the side.

Serves 6

Chicken chasseur

1 kg (2 lb 4 oz) chicken thigh fillets
2 tablespoons oil
1 garlic clove, crushed
1 large onion, sliced
100 g (3½ oz) button mushrooms,
    sliced
1 teaspoon thyme leaves
400 g (14 oz) tinned chopped
    tomatoes
60 ml (2 fl oz/¼ cup) chicken stock
60 ml (2 fl oz/¼ cup) white wine
1 tablespoon tomato paste
    (concentrated purée)

Preheat the oven to 180°C (350°F/ Gas 4). Trim chicken of excess fat and sinew. Heat oil in a heavy-based frying pan and brown the chicken in batches over medium heat. Drain on paper towels. Transfer to a casserole dish.

Add garlic, onion and mushrooms to the pan and cook over medium heat for 5 minutes, or until soft. Add to chicken with the thyme and tomatoes.

Combine the stock, wine and tomato paste and pour over the chicken. Bake, covered, for 1¼ hours, or until the chicken is tender.

Serves 4

Braised beef in red wine

30 g (1 oz/¼ cup) plain (all-purpose)
  flour
¼ teaspoon ground black pepper
1 kg (2 lb 4 oz) lean round or chuck
  steak, cut into 3 cm (1¼ in) cubes
1 tablespoon oil
15 g (½ oz) butter
12 baby onions
250 ml (9 fl oz/1 cup) beef stock
250 ml (9 fl oz/1 cup) red wine
2 tablespoons tomato paste
  (concentrated purée)
1 tablespoon French mustard
1 bay leaf
¼ teaspoon mixed dried herbs

Combine flour and pepper. Toss the meat in the seasoned flour, shaking off the excess.

Heat oil and butter in a heavy-based saucepan. Cook the meat quickly in batches over medium–high heat until well browned. Drain on paper towels.

Add the onions to the pan and cook over medium heat until golden brown. Return meat to the pan and stir in the stock, wine, tomato paste, mustard and the herbs. Bring to the boil, then reduce the heat and simmer, covered, for 1½ hours, or until meat is tender, stirring occasionally.

Serves 6

Stewed lentils with chorizo

400 g (14 oz) green lentils
100 ml (3½ fl oz) olive oil
2 garlic cloves, crushed
1 green capsicum (pepper), seeded
    and diced
2 brown onions, chopped
2 teaspoons sweet paprika (pimentón)
1 bay leaf
2 bacon slices, cut into thin strips
200 g (7 oz) chorizo, sliced
1 tomato, chopped
extra virgin olive oil, for drizzling

Rinse the lentils, then cover with cold water and soak for 2 hours.

Heat 1 tablespoon of the olive oil in a large saucepan over medium heat and cook garlic, capsicum and half the onion for 5 minutes, or until the onion is softened. Add drained lentils, paprika, bay leaf and most of the remaining oil. Cover with water, bring to the boil, then reduce the heat and simmer for 30 minutes, or until tender.

Meanwhile, heat the remaining oil in a frying pan. Add the bacon, chorizo and remaining onion and then fry for 10 minutes until golden on medium heat. Add to the lentil mixture with the tomato and a large pinch of salt, and cook for another 5 minutes. Drizzle a little extra virgin olive oil over the top and serve.

Serves 4

Chicken cacciatore

3 tablespoons olive oil
1 large onion, finely chopped
3 garlic cloves, crushed
1 celery stalk, finely chopped
150 g (5½ oz) pancetta, finely
    chopped
125 g (4½ oz) button mushrooms,
    thickly sliced
4 chicken drumsticks
4 chicken thighs
90 ml (3 fl oz) dry vermouth or dry
    white wine
800 g (1 lb 12 oz) tinned chopped
    tomatoes
¼ teaspoon sugar
1 oregano sprig, plus 4–5 sprigs,
    to garnish
1 rosemary sprig
1 bay leaf

Heat half the oil in a casserole. Add the onion, garlic, celery and pancetta and cook, stirring occasionally, over low heat for 6–8 minutes.

Add mushrooms, increase the heat and cook, stirring occasionally, for 4–5 minutes. Spoon out onto a plate and set aside.

Add the remaining olive oil to the casserole and then brown the chicken piece. Season to taste. Spoon off any excess fat and return all the pieces to the casserole. Add vermouth or wine, increase the heat and cook until liquid has almost evaporated.

Stir in the tomatoes, sugar, oregano, rosemary, bay leaf and 75 ml cold water. Bring everything to the boil, then stir in reserved pancetta mixture. Cover, turn down the heat and leave to simmer for 30 minutes, or until the chicken is tender.

If the liquid is too thin, remove the chicken from the casserole, increase the heat and boil until the sauce has thickened. Discard the sprigs of herbs and season. Return the chicken to the casserole and add additional oregano sprigs before serving.

Serves 4

Asturian stew

400 g (14 oz/2 cups) dried white
 haricot beans (such as navy beans)
700 g (1 lb 9 oz) smoked ham hock
2 tablespoons olive oil
150 g (5½ oz) bacon, chopped
1 brown onion, chopped
2 garlic cloves, chopped
pinch of saffron threads
1 teaspoon sweet paprika (pimentón)
1 bay leaf
200 g (7 oz) morcilla blood sausages,
 sliced

Rinse the beans and soak overnight in cold water.

Put ham hock in a large saucepan and cover with water. Bring to the boil, then reduce heat and simmer for at least 1 hour, or until meat is tender and starting to come away from the bone. Allow to cool, then remove the meat from the bone and cut into 2 cm (³/₄ in) cubes. Reserve about 1 litre (35 fl oz/4 cups) of the cooking liquid.

Heat the oil in a large, heavy-based saucepan and cook the bacon, onion and the garlic for 5 minutes or until translucent. Add beans, cubed ham, saffron, paprika and bay leaf, and then season to taste.

Add the reserved cooking liquid, bring to the boil, then reduce the heat and simmer for at least 1 hour, or until the beans are cooked (they need to be soft but not mushy). Add the morcilla and then cook for 5 minutes, or until heated through. Season.

Serves 4

Beef stroganoff

1 kg (2 lb 4 oz) piece rump steak,
trimmed
40 g (1½ oz/⅓ cup) plain
(all-purpose) flour
¼ teaspoon ground black pepper
60 ml (2 fl oz/¼ cup) olive oil
1 large onion, chopped
500 g (1 lb 2 oz) baby mushrooms
1 tablespoon sweet paprika
1 tablespoon tomato paste
2 teaspoons French mustard
125 ml (4 fl oz/½ cup) dry white wine
60 ml (2 fl oz/¼ cup) chicken stock
185 g (6½ oz/¾ cup) sour cream
1 tablespoon finely chopped parsley

Slice meat across grain into short, thin pieces. Combine the flour and pepper. Toss meat in the seasoned flour and shake off the excess.

Heat 2 tablespoons of oil in a heavy-based saucepan. Cook meat quickly in small batches over medium–high heat until well browned, then drain on paper towels.

Heat the remaining oil in the pan. Cook the onion over medium heat for 3 minutes, or until soft. Add the mushrooms and stir for 5 minutes.

Add paprika, tomato paste, mustard, wine and stock to the pan, and bring to the boil. Reduce heat and simmer for 5 minutes, uncovered, stirring occasionally. Return the meat to the pan with the sour cream, and stir until combined and just heated through. Sprinkle with parsley before serving.

Serves 6

Chicken paprika

800 g (1 lb 10 oz) chicken thigh fillets
60 g (2¼ oz) plain (all-purpose) flour
2 tablespoons oil
2 onions, chopped
1–2 garlic cloves, crushed
2 tablespoons sweet paprika
125 ml (4 fl oz/½ cup) red wine
1 tablespoon tomato paste
  (concentrated purée)
425 g (14 oz) tinned tomatoes
200 g (7 oz) button mushrooms
125 ml (4 fl oz/½ cup) chicken stock
80 g (2¾ oz/⅔ cup) sour cream

Rinse the chicken and dry well. Trim the chicken of excess fat and sinew. Cut the chicken into 3 cm (1¼ inch) pieces. Season the flour with salt and pepper. Toss the chicken pieces lightly in the seasoned flour, shake off the excess and reserve the flour. Heat half the oil in a large heavy-based pan. Cook the chicken pieces quickly in small batches over medium-high heat. Remove from the pan and drain on paper towels.

Heat remaining oil in pan and add the onion and garlic. Cook, stirring, until the onion is soft. Add paprika and the reserved flour, and stir for 1 minute. Add chicken, wine, tomato paste and undrained crushed tomatoes. Bring to the boil, reduce the heat and simmer, covered, for 15 minutes.

Add the mushrooms and chicken stock. Simmer, covered, for a further 10 minutes. Add the sour cream and stir until heated through, but do not allow to boil.

Serves 4–6

Coq au vin

2 x 1.6 kg (3 lb 8 oz) whole chicken
750 ml (26 fl oz/3 cups) red wine
2 bay leaves
2 thyme sprigs
250 g (9 oz) bacon slices, diced
60 g (2¼ oz) butter
20 baby onions
250 g (9 oz) button mushrooms
1 teaspoon oil
30 g (1 oz) plain (all-purpose) flour
1 litre (35 fl oz/4 cups) chicken stock
125 ml (4 fl oz/½ cup) brandy
2 teaspoons tomato paste
  (concentrated purée)
30 g (1 oz) butter, softened
1 tablespoon plain (all-purpose) flour
2 tablespoons chopped flat-leaf
  (Italian) parsley

Joint each chicken into eight pieces by removing both legs and cutting between joint of drumstick and thigh. Cut down either side of the backbone and lift it out. Turn over and then cut through cartilage down the centre of breastbone. Cut each breast in half, leaving wing attached to top half.

Put wine, bay leaves, thyme and salt and pepper in a bowl and add the chicken. Cover and refrigerate for 4 hours, or overnight. Blanch bacon in boiling water and sauté in a frying pan until brown. Lift out onto a plate. Melt 15 g (½ oz) of butter in pan, add onions and sauté until browned. Lift out and set aside. Melt a further 15 g (½ oz) of butter, add the mushrooms, season and then sauté for 5 minutes. Remove and set aside. Drain chicken, reserving marinade, and pat dry. Add butter and oil to frying pan, add the chicken and then sauté until golden. Stir in flour.

Transfer chicken to a saucepan and add stock. Pour brandy into frying pan and boil, stirring, for 30 seconds to deglaze pan. Pour over chicken. Add marinade, onions, mushrooms, bacon and tomato paste. Cook over medium heat for 45 minutes, or until chicken is cooked through.

Serves 8

Chicken with feta and olives

2 tablespoons oil
8 (1.2 kg/2 lb 12 oz) chicken pieces
1 onion, chopped
25 g (1 oz) oregano, leaves picked
2 tablespoons tomato paste
  (concentrated purée)
850 g (1 lb 14 oz) tinned crushed
  tomatoes
150 g (5½ oz) black olives
150 g (5½ oz) feta cheese, crumbled

Heat half the oil in a saucepan and cook chicken pieces, in batches, for 3–4 minutes, or until golden brown. Remove from the pan and set aside.

In the same saucepan, heat remaining oil and cook the onion and half the oregano leaves for 3 minutes, or until onion is soft. Add the tomato paste to onion mixture and stir for 2 minutes, then add tomato and chicken pieces.

Simmer, covered, for 40–50 minutes, or until chicken is cooked through. Add the remaining oregano leaves and the olives. To serve, spoon into bowls and top with crumbled feta.

Serves 4

Afelia (Cypriot pork and coriander stew)

1 ½ tablespoons coriander seeds
½ teaspoon cracked black pepper
800 g (1 lb 10 oz) pork fillet, cut into
    2 cm (¾ inch) dice
1 tablespoon plain (all-purpose) flour
60 ml (2 fl oz/¼ cup) olive oil
1 large onion, thinly sliced
375 ml (12 fl oz/1 ½ cups) red wine
250 ml (9 fl oz/1 cup) chicken stock
1 teaspoon sugar
coriander (cilantro) sprigs, to garnish

Crush coriander seeds in a mortar and pestle. Transfer to a bowl, add the cracked black pepper and the pork and toss to coat. Cover and refrigerate overnight.

Add flour to the pork and toss. Heat 2 tablespoons oil in a frying pan and cook the pork in batches over high heat for 1–2 minutes, or until brown. Remove from the pan.

Heat remaining oil in the pan, add the onion and cook over medium heat for 2–3 minutes, or until golden. Return meat to the pan, add red wine, stock and sugar. Season, bring to the boil, then reduce the heat and simmer, covered, for 1 hour.

Remove the meat. Return pan to the heat and then boil over high heat for 3–5 minutes, or until the sauce is reduced and slightly thickened. Pour over the meat and then garnish with coriander sprigs.

Serves 4–6

Lamb caldereta

2 tablespoons olive oil
1 brown onion, roughly diced
1 carrot, roughly diced
1 red capsicum (pepper), cut into
   large dice
2 garlic cloves, chopped
1 kg (2 lb 4 oz) lamb leg, boned and
   cut into 2 cm (³/₄ in) cubes
1 ham bone or trimmings
400 g (14 oz) tinned chopped
   tomatoes
2 tablespoons chopped flat-leaf
   (Italian) parsley
2 tablespoons chopped mint
2 tablespoons tomato paste
   (concentrated purée)
2 bay leaves
250 ml (9 fl oz/1 cup) white wine
1 teaspoon ground cumin
1 teaspoon sweet paprika (pimentón)
25 g (1 oz/¹/₄ cup) dry breadcrumbs
¹/₂ teaspoon ground cinnamon

Preheat oven to 180°C (350°F/Gas 4).
Heat the olive oil in a large flameproof
casserole dish over medium heat and
cook the onion, carrot, capsicum and
the garlic for about 8 minutes, until
softened. Add lamb cubes, ham bone
or trimmings, tomato, parsley, mint,
tomato paste, bay leaves, white wine
and 185 ml (6 fl oz/³/₄ cup) water.
Bring to the boil, then cover and bake
for about 1–1¹/₂ hours, or until tender.

Meanwhile, combine cumin, paprika,
breadcrumbs, cinnamon and a pinch
of pepper.

Remove the lamb from the casserole
dish with a slotted spoon or tongs
and set aside. Discard the bay leaves
and ham bone. Purée the remaining
liquid and vegetables, then stir in the
breadcrumb mixture. Cook, stirring,
for 10 minutes, or until the sauce has
thickened. Return lamb to casserole
and gently warm through. Season to
taste. Serve with green beans.

Serves 4

Venison casserole

1 rosemary sprig
1 large onion
1 garlic clove
85 g (3 oz) prosciutto
100 g (3½ oz) butter
1 kg (2 lb 4 oz) venison, cut into
  large cubes
1 litre (35 fl oz/4 cups) beef stock
80 ml (2½ fl oz/⅓ cup) red wine
  vinegar
80 ml (2½ fl oz/⅓ cup) robust red
  wine
2 cloves
4 juniper berries
pinch of allspice
1 bay leaf
3 tablespoons plain (all-purpose) flour
2 tablespoons dry Marsala or brandy
1½ teaspoons grated lemon zest
1½ tablespoons finely chopped
  parsley

Strip the leaves off the rosemary and chop them finely with the onion, garlic and prosciutto. Heat half the butter in a heavy saucepan with a lid. Add the chopped mixture and soften over low heat for 5 minutes. Season with pepper. Increase the heat, add the venison and cook for 10 minutes, or until brown on all sides. put the stock in another saucepan and bring to the boil, then reduce the heat and keep at a low simmer.

Increase the heat under the venison, add the vinegar and cook until thick. Pour in red wine. When that becomes syrupy, stir in half of the simmering stock. Add the cloves, juniper berries, allspice and bay leaf and cover the pan. Simmer for 1 hour, stirring once or twice.

Meanwhile, melt the remaining butter in a saucepan. Stir in flour and cook over low heat for 1 minute. Slowly stir in the remaining stock and cook until the sauce thickens slightly.

Stir the sauce into the venison casserole, then add Marsala. Uncover the pan and then simmer for a further 20 minutes. Mix together lemon zest and parsley and sprinkle over the top before serving.

Serves 4

Stifado

4 tablespoons olive oil
1.8 kg (4 lb) round or chuck beef, in
3 cm (1 in) cubes
1 teaspoon ground cumin
2 onions, finely chopped
3 garlic cloves, crushed
250 ml (9 fl oz/1 cup) dry red wine
3 tablespoons tomato paste
(concentrated purée)
4 tablespoons red wine vinegar
2 cinnamon sticks
10 cloves
2 bay leaves
2 teaspoons sugar
1 kg (2 lb 4 oz) pickling onions
4 tablespoons currants
200 g (7 oz) feta cheese, cut into
small cubes

Heat half the oil in a large flameproof casserole dish and brown the beef in batches, adding more oil as needed. Put the beef in a bowl, then sprinkle with the cumin and set aside. Add more oil and soften the onions and garlic over a low heat for 5–6 minutes. Return the meat to the pot.

Stir in the wine, increase the heat and deglaze the pot. Add 500 ml (17 fl oz/ 2 cups) of water, the tomato paste and wine vinegar and bring to the boil. Add the cinnamon, cloves, bay leaves and sugar, and season with salt and freshly ground black pepper. Reduce the heat, cover with a double layer of foil and put the lid on. Simmer over a very low heat for 1 hour.

Peel the onions and cut a cross in the base. Add to the pot along with the currants. Continue cooking for a further 1½ hours, or until the beef is very tender and the sauce is thick. Discard the cinnamon sticks and bay leaves. Stir the cheese in and simmer for 3–4 minutes, uncovered. Taste for seasoning and serve straight from the pot. Serve with rice.

Serves 6–8

Pork, beer and chickpea stew

2 teaspoons ground cumin
1 teaspoon ground coriander
½ teaspoon chilli powder
½ teaspoon ground cinnamon
400 g (14 oz) lean diced pork, trimmed
1 tablespoon plain (all-purpose) flour
1 tablespoon olive oil
1 large onion, finely chopped
3 garlic cloves, finely chopped
2 large carrots, finely chopped
2 celery stalks, thinly sliced
125 ml (4 fl oz/½ cup) chicken stock
125 ml (4 fl oz/½ cup) beer
2 ripe tomatoes, chopped
310 g (11 oz) tinned chickpeas, rinsed
2 tablespoons chopped parsley

Cook the spices in a dry frying pan over low heat, shaking the pan, for 1 minute, or until aromatic.

Combine pork with the spices and flour in a plastic bag and toss well. Remove the pork and shake off the excess flour. Heat oil in a large heavy-based saucepan over high heat and cook the pork, tossing regularly, for 8 minutes, or until lightly browned.

Add onion, garlic, carrot, celery and half the stock to pan and toss well. Cover and cook for 10 minutes. Add the remaining stock, beer and tomato and season to taste. Bring to the boil, reduce the heat, cover with a tight-fitting lid, then simmer over low heat for 1 hour. Gently shake pan every now and then, but do not remove the lid during cooking. Stir in chickpeas and parsley. Simmer, uncovered, for 5 minutes and serve.

Serves 4

Rich steak and kidney stew

1 kg (2 lb 4 oz) chuck steak
2–3 tablespoons oil
1 thick bacon slice, rind removed
  and thinly sliced
40 g (11/2 oz) butter
1 large onion, chopped
300 g (101/2 oz) button mushrooms
250 ml (9 fl oz/1 cup) brown muscat
  or sweet dessert wine
2–3 garlic cloves, crushed
1/4 teaspoon ground allspice
1/2 teaspoon paprika
2 teaspoons coriander (cilantro)
  seeds, lightly crushed
8 lamb kidneys (425 g/15 oz),
  quartered, cores removed
1 tablespoon wholegrain mustard
250 ml (9 fl oz/1 cup) beef or
  vegetable stock
2–3 tablespoons soft brown sugar
1–2 teaspoons thyme
1–2 teaspoons rosemary

Trim steak of excess fat and sinew; cut into 2–3 cm (3/4–11/2 in) cubes. Heat 1 teaspoon of oil in a heavy-based pan. Add bacon and cook for 2–3 minutes until crisp; remove. Add 2 tablespoons oil and 30 g (1 oz) butter to pan. Brown steak in batches in hot oil, then remove from pan and set aside. Add onion to pan and cook for 2–3 minutes until soft and golden.

Add mushrooms and cook, stirring, for 3 minutes, until brown. Stir in half the muscat and simmer for around 3–4 minutes. Remove from pan. Add remaining oil and butter to pan. Stir in garlic, allspice, paprika and coriander seeds and then cook for 1 minute.

Add kidneys and cook, stirring, over medium heat until just beginning to brown. Stir in remaining muscat and mustard and simmer for 2 minutes. Return mushroom and onion mixture to pan, with steak and bacon, and stir until combined. Stir in stock. Bring to the boil, reduce heat, cover and then simmer for 1 hour. Stir in sugar (the amount depends on the sweetness of the muscat), cover and simmer for 40 minutes. Uncover and then simmer for 20 minutes. Stir in the thyme and the rosemary.

Serves 4–6

Caldo gallego

250 g (9 oz/1¼ cups) white haricot
  beans, such as navy beans
500 g (1 lb 2 oz) smoked ham hock
2 tablespoons olive oil
1 leek, washed and chopped
1 garlic clove, chopped
500 g (1 lb 2 oz) pork babyback or,
  separated into 5 cm (2 in) widths
  American-style ribs
2 potatoes, peeled and cubed
1 bay leaf
1 kg (2 lb 4 oz) silverbeet (Swiss
  chard), washed well and chopped

Rinse beans, then soak them in cold water for at least 5 hours. Put ham hock in a heavy-based saucepan and cover with cold water. Bring to the boil, then reduce the heat and simmer for about 1 hour, or until meat starts to come away from the bone and is tender. Allow hock to cool. When cool enough to handle, remove meat from bone and cut into 2 cm (³/₄ in) cubes. Reserve 625 ml (22 fl oz/2½ cups) of cooking liquid.

Put the beans in a saucepan and cover them with cold water. Bring to the boil, then reduce the heat and simmer for 30 minutes, or until tender. Drain, reserving 250 ml (9 fl oz/1 cup) of the cooking liquid.

Heat the olive oil in a large heavy-based saucepan over medium heat and cook leek and garlic for about 5 minutes, or until translucent. Add the ham, beans, ribs, potato, bay leaf and reserved cups of cooking liquid (you need to make sure the food is covered with liquid).

Bring to the boil, then reduce the heat, cover simmer for 45 minutes. Stir in the silverbeet and cook for a further 5 minutes. Season to taste.

Serves 4

Lamb with quince

1.5 kg (3 lb) lamb shoulder, cut into 3 cm
  (1¼ inch) pieces
2 large onions, diced
½ teaspoon ground ginger
½ teaspoon cayenne pepper
¼ teaspoon pulverised saffron threads
1 teaspoon ground coriander
1 cinnamon stick
½ cup (25 g/¾ oz) roughly chopped
  fresh coriander
40 g (1¼ oz) butter
500 g (1 lb) quinces, peeled, cored
  and quartered
100 g (3½ oz) dried apricots
fresh coriander sprigs, extra, to garnish

Place the lamb in a heavy-based, flameproof casserole dish and add half the onion, the ginger, cayenne pepper, saffron, ground coriander, cinnamon stick, fresh coriander and some salt and pepper. Cover with cold water and bring to the boil over medium heat and simmer, partly covered, for 1½ hours, or until the lamb is tender.

While lamb is cooking, melt the butter in a heavy-based frying pan and cook the remaining onion and the quinces for 15 minutes over medium heat, or until lightly golden.

When the lamb has been cooking for 1 hour, add the quinces and apricots.

Taste sauce and adjust seasoning if necessary. Transfer to a warm serving dish and sprinkle with the coriander sprigs. Serve with couscous or rice.

Serves 4–6

Kashmir lamb with spinach

2 tablespoons oil
750 g (1 lb 10 oz) diced leg of lamb
2 large onions, chopped
3 garlic cloves, crushed
5 cm (2 in) piece fresh ginger, grated
2 teaspoons ground cumin
2 teaspoons ground coriander
2 teaspoons turmeric
1/2 teaspoon ground cardamom
1/2 teaspoon ground cloves
3 bay leaves
375 ml (13 fl oz/1 1/2 cups) chicken
  stock
125 ml (4 fl oz/1/2 cup) cream
2 bunches English spinach leaves,
  washed and chopped

Heat the oil in a heavy-based pan and brown lamb in batches. Remove from pan. Add onion, garlic and ginger and cook for 3 minutes, stirring regularly. Add the cumin, coriander, turmeric, cardamom and cloves and then cook, stirring, for 1–2 minutes, or until fragrant. Return lamb to the pan with any juices. Add bay leaves and stock.

Bring to the boil and then reduce the heat, stir well, cover and simmer for 35 minutes. Add the cream and cook, covered, for a further 20 minutes or until the lamb is very tender.

Add the spinach and cook until it has softened. Season to taste.

Serves 4

Rabbit in red wine

2 x 1 kg (2 lb 4 oz) rabbits, jointed
  and cut into 8 pieces each
100 ml (3½ fl oz) olive oil
1 large brown onion, chopped
6 roma (plum) tomatoes, peeled and
  chopped
1 teaspoon sweet paprika (pimentón)
6 garlic cloves, crushed
3 slices jamón or prosciutto, cut into
  strips
100 g (3½ oz) chorizo, chopped
3 red capsicums (peppers), seeded
  and diced
2 tablespoons chopped thyme
250 ml (9 fl oz/1 cup) red wine
1 handful flat-leaf (Italian) parsley,
  chopped

Season the rabbit pieces. Heat half
the oil in a heavy-based flameproof
casserole dish over medium heat,
add rabbit in batches and cook for
about 4 minutes per batch, or until
golden. Remove and set aside.

Heat the rest of the oil in the dish
and cook the onion for 5 minutes,
or until softened. Add the tomato
and simmer gently for 10 minutes.
Stir in the paprika, garlic, jamón,
chorizo, capsicum, thyme, red wine,
rabbit pieces and 2 tablespoons of
the parsley. Check the seasoning.
Bring to the boil, then reduce the
heat and simmer for 35 minutes,
or until the rabbit is tender.

Remove rabbit pieces and simmer
the sauce for 20–30 minutes, or until
it has reduced and slightly thickened.
Return rabbit to the casserole and
gently heat through. Season to taste,
garnish with the parsley and serve.

Serves 4

Chicken with forty cloves of garlic

2 celery stalks, including leaves
2 rosemary sprigs, plus extra to garnish
4 thyme sprigs, plus extra to garnish
4 flat-leaf (Italian) parsley sprigs, plus extra to garnish
1.6 kg (3 lb 8 oz) whole chicken
40 garlic cloves, unpeeled
2 tablespoons olive oil
1 carrot, roughly chopped
1 small onion, cut into 4 wedges
250 ml (9 fl oz/1 cup) white wine
1 baguette, cut into slices

Preheat the oven to 200°C (400°F/ Gas 6). Put a chopped celery stalk and 2 sprigs each of the rosemary, thyme and parsley into the chicken cavity. Add 6 garlic cloves. Tie the legs together and tuck the wing tips under. Brush the chicken with some oil and season well. Scatter about 10 more garlic cloves in a saucepan. Put remaining sprigs of herbs, chopped celery, carrot and onion in the saucepan.

Put chicken into saucepan. Scatter the remaining garlic cloves around the chicken and add the remaining oil and the wine. Cover and bake for 1 hour 20 minutes.

Lift the chicken out of the saucepan. Drain juices into a saucepan. Remove garlic cloves from the drained mixture and set aside. Spoon off fat from the juices and boil to reduce and thicken.

Cut chicken into portions, pour over a little of the juices and scatter with the garlic. Toast the baguette slices, then spread with the soft flesh squeezed from the garlic. Garnish the chicken with herb sprigs and serve with the baguette slices.

Serves 4

Lemon and rosemary chicken stew

8 large chicken drumsticks
60 g (2¼ oz) butter
2 garlic cloves, crushed
2 teaspoons finely grated lemon zest
2 tablespoons chopped rosemary
1 tablespoon plain (all-purpose) flour
375 ml (12 fl oz/1½ cups) chicken
  stock
2 tablespoons lemon juice

Using a knife, make two deep cuts in the thickest part of each chicken drumstick.

Melt the butter in a large frying pan. Add the drumsticks and cook over medium heat for 2 minutes on each side, or until brown. Add the garlic, lemon rind and rosemary.

Blend flour, stock and lemon juice until smooth. Add to the pan and bring to the boil. Reduce heat and simmer, covered, for 25 minutes, or until the drumsticks are tender, stirring occasionally. Season.

Serves 4

Note: To check whether chicken is cooked, insert a skewer into the thickest part. If the juice runs clear, the chicken is cooked.

Cochifrito

80 ml (2½ fl oz/⅓ cup) olive oil
1 kg (2 lb 4 oz) lamb shoulder, diced
1 large onion, finely chopped
4 garlic cloves, crushed
2 teaspoons sweet pimentón (paprika)
80 ml (2½ fl oz/⅓ cup) lemon juice,
    plus 1 tablespoon, extra
2 tablespoons flat-leaf (Italian) parsley

Heat oil in a large, heavy-based deep frying pan over high heat and cook lamb in 2 batches for 5 minutes each batch, or until well browned. Remove all the lamb from the pan.

Add onion to the pan and cook for 4–5 minutes, or until soft and golden. Stir in garlic and paprika and cook for 1 minute. Return the lamb to the pan with the lemon juice and 1.75 litres (61 fl oz/7 cups) water. Gently simmer over low heat, stirring occasionally, for 2 hours, or until the liquid has almost evaporated and oil starts to reappear. Stir in the parsley and the extra lemon juice, season with salt and freshly ground black pepper and serve.

Serves 4–6

Lamb and mustard stew

750 g (1 lb 10 oz) lean lamb fillets, cut
   into 2.5 cm (1 in) cubes
60 g (2¼ oz/½ cup) plain (all-
   purpose) flour
1 tablespoon oil
16 baby onions
250 ml (9 fl oz/1 cup) white wine
250 ml (9 fl oz/1 cup) chicken stock
125 g (4½ oz/½ cup) Dijon mustard
2 tablespoons chopped thyme

Toss lamb cubes in flour, shaking off any excess. Heat oil in a heavy-based saucepan over high heat. Add lamb in small batches and cook for 3 minutes, or until browned, turning occasionally. Drain lamb on paper towels.

Return lamb to pan. Add the onions, wine, stock, mustard and the thyme. Bring to the boil, then reduce heat to low and simmer, covered, for 1 hour, stirring occasionally. Remove lid and simmer for another 30 minutes, or until lamb is tender. Serve with pasta.

Serves 4

Note: A small, boned leg of lamb is ideal for this dish.

Spanish pork and vegetable stew

600 g (1lb 5 oz) boneless pork
  shoulder (hand/collar butt)
4 (100 g/3½ oz each) all-purpose
  potatoes, peeled
1 red capsicum (pepper)
1 green capsicum (pepper)
2 tablespoons olive oil
1 large red onion, chopped
2 garlic cloves, crushed
100 g (3½ oz) jamón
1 chorizo, sliced
800g (1lb 12 oz) tinned tomatoes,
  chopped
10 g (¼ oz) thyme
2 tablespoons sherry vinegar
100 ml (3½ fl oz) white wine
1 bay leaf
250 ml (9 fl oz/1 cup) chicken stock

Cut the pork into 2 cm (¾ in) pieces. Peel the potatoes and cut into same size. Seed and chop capsicums into 2 cm (¾ in) squares.

Preheat oven to 180°C (350°F/Gas 4). Place a large frying pan over medium heat. Heat the oil then add the pork, onions and garlic. Cook for 5 minutes until onion is softened and meat is lightly browned all over. Add chorizo, capsicums and jamón. Continue to cook, stirring, for another 5 minutes or until slightly reduced.

Place in a large, deep ovenproof pan or casserole dish. Add the rest of the ingredients and season with salt and pepper. Place in oven and cook for 2 hours or until meat is very tender.

Serves 4–6

Chicken in samfaina sauce

1.5 kg (3 lb 5 oz) chicken, cut into
    8 pieces
60 ml (2 fl oz/¼ cup) olive oil
2 large brown onions, chopped
400 g (14 oz) eggplant (aubergine),
    peeled and cut into 2 cm (³/₄ in)
    cubes
3 garlic cloves, crushed
350 g (12 oz) zucchini (courgettes),
    cut into strips
2 green or red capsicums (peppers),
    cut into 1 cm (½ in) strips
800 g (1 lb 12 oz) tinned chopped
    tomatoes
1 bay leaf
2 tablespoons chopped herbs, such
    as thyme, oregano and flat-leaf
    (Italian) parsley
125 ml (4 fl oz/½ cup) white wine

Season chicken pieces with salt and
pepper. Heat the oil in a large heavy-
based saucepan over medium heat,
add chicken in batches and brown
well on all sides. Remove from pan
and reduce the heat to low–medium.

Add the onion and cook for about
10 minutes, or until softened. Add
the eggplant, garlic, zucchini and
capsicum and cook for 10 minutes,
or until the vegetables are softened.

Stir in the tomato, bay leaf, herbs and
wine, and return the chicken pieces to
the pan. Bring to the boil, then cover
and simmer over low heat for about
45 minutes, or until chicken is tender
and the eggplant is soft. Season well
with salt and pepper before serving.

Serves 4

Beef and vegetable casserole

500 g (1 lb 2 oz) lean round steak
cooking oil spray
1 onion, sliced
3 garlic cloves, crushed
2 teaspoons ground cumin
1 teaspoon dried thyme leaves
2 bay leaves
400 g (14 oz) tinned chopped
  tomatoes
500 g (1 lb 2 oz) potatoes, chopped
2 large carrots, thickly sliced
4 zucchini (courgettes), thickly sliced
250 g (9 oz) mushrooms, halved
250 g (9 oz) yellow squash, halved
2 tablespoons tomato paste
  (concentrated purée)
125 ml (4 fl oz/½ cup) red wine
3 large handfuls parsley, chopped

Preheat the oven to 180°C (350°F/ Gas 4). Remove any excess fat and sinew from the meat and cut into 2 cm (³/₄ inch) cubes. Spray a deep, non-stick frying pan with oil and fry the meat in batches until brown. Remove from the pan. Spray the pan again, add the onion and cook until lightly golden. Add the garlic, cumin, thyme and bay leaves and stir for 1 minute.

Return the meat and any juices to the pan, tossing to coat with spices. Add 375 ml (13 fl oz/1½ cups) water and tomato, scraping the pan. Simmer for 10 minutes, or until thickened. Mix in a large casserole dish along with the vegetables, tomato paste and wine.

Bake, covered, for 1 hour. Stir well, then uncover and bake for a further 20 minutes. Season, remove the bay leaves and stir in the parsley.

Serves 6

Pork sausage and white bean stew

350 g (11 oz) dried white haricot
  beans
150 g (5½ oz) tocino, speck or
  pancetta, unsliced
½ leek, thinly sliced
2 garlic cloves
1 bay leaf
1 small fresh red chilli, halved and
  seeded
1 small onion
2 cloves
1 rosemary sprig
3 thyme sprigs
1 parsley sprig
60 ml (2 fl oz/¼ cup) olive oil
8 pork sausages
½ onion, finely chopped
1 green capsicum (pepper), finely
  chopped
½ teaspoon paprika
125 ml (4 fl oz/½ cup) tomato purée
1 teaspoon cider vinegar

Soak beans overnight in cold water. Drain and rinser. Put in a saucepan with tocino, leek, garlic, bay leaf and chilli. Stud the onion with the cloves and add to saucepan. Tie rosemary, thyme and the parsley together, and add to pan. Pour in 750 ml (26 fl oz/ 3 cups) water and bring to the boil. Add 1 tablespoon of oil, reduce the heat and then simmer, covered, for about 1 hour.

Prick each sausage 5 times and then twist tightly in opposite directions in middle to create 2 short fat sausages joined in middle. Put in a single layer in a frying pan and add enough cold water to reach halfway up their sides. Bring to the boil and simmer, turning, until all the water has evaporated and the sausages brown. Remove and cut the short sausages apart. Add the remaining oil, onion and capsicum to the pan, and fry over medium heat for 5–6 minutes. Stir in paprika, cook for 30 seconds, then add tomato purée. Season. Cook, stirring, for 1 minute.

Remove tocino and herb sprigs from the bean mixture. Add sausages and sauce to the pan, and stir the vinegar through. Bring to the boil.

Serves 4

Beef bourguignon

1 kg (2 lb 4 oz) lean topside or
  round steak
plain (all-purpose) flour, for dusting
50 g (1³/₄ oz) low-fat back bacon
2 teaspoons olive or canola oil
12 baby onions
250 ml (9 fl oz/1 cup) red wine
500 ml (17 fl oz/2 cups) beef stock
1 teaspoon dried thyme
200 g (7 oz) button mushrooms
2 bay leaves
375 g (13 oz) fettucine

Trim steak and cut into 2 cm (³/₄ in) cubes. Season the flour with salt and freshly ground black pepper. Lightly toss the steak in the flour, shaking off the excess.

Cut bacon into 2 cm (³/₄ in) squares. Heat the oil in a large heavy-based saucepan and briefly cook the bacon over medium heat. Remove the bacon from pan, then add meat and brown well. Remove and set aside. Add the onions to pan and cook until golden.

Return bacon and meat to the pan with the remaining ingredients. Bring to the boil, reduce heat and simmer, covered, for 1½ hours, or until meat is very tender, stirring occasionally. Remove the bay leaves.

Meanwhile, cook pasta in a saucepan of boiling water for about 10 minutes, or until *al dente*. Drain well. Serve with the beef.

Serves 6

Creamy veal and mushroom stew

750 g (1½ lb) veal steaks, cut into
  1 cm (½ in) strips
30 g (1 oz) plain (all-purpose) flour
30 g (1 oz) butter
1 garlic clove, crushed
1 tablespoon dijon mustard
250 ml (9 fl oz/1 cup) cream
125 ml (4 fl oz/½ cup) white wine
1 tablespoon chopped thyme
250 ml (9 fl oz/1 cup) chicken stock
375 g (12 oz) button mushrooms,
  halved

Toss meat in the flour, shaking off the excess. Heat the butter and garlic in a heavy-based saucepan. Add the meat and cook quickly in small batches over medium heat until well browned. Drain on paper towels.

Return meat to the pan and add mustard, cream, wine, thyme and stock. Bring to the boil, then reduce the heat and simmer, covered, for 1½ hours, stirring occasionally.

Add the mushrooms and cook for a further 15 minutes, or until the meat is tender. Delicious served with pasta and steamed vegetables.

Serves 4

Italian-style spicy sausage and bean casserole

300 g (10½ oz) dried cannellini beans
300 g (10½ oz) dried black-eyed
    beans
1 tablespoon olive oil
6 large country pork sausages
6 rashers rindless streaky bacon, cut
    into 6–7 cm (2–3 in) lengths
4 small onions, quartered from top
    to bottom
10 whole garlic cloves, peeled
3 long thin carrots, cut into 3 cm (1 in)
    sections
3 bay leaves
7 oregano sprigs, leaves only
1 small red chilli, split and deseeded
500 ml (17 fl oz/2 cups) chicken stock
2 tablespoons tomato paste
    (concentrated purée)

Cover the beans with plenty of cold water and soak overnight. Drain and rinse under cold water. Put in a large stockpot or flameproof casserole dish and cover with cold water. Bring to the boil and simmer for 30 minutes. Drain and reserve until needed.

Heat the oil in the pot and lightly brown sausages for 4–5 minutes. Remove and reserve. Take pot off the heat and layer the bacon over the base. Add the onions, garlic and carrots and season well with freshly ground black pepper. Put sausages on top. Add the bay leaves, half the oregano and chilli. Cover with beans.

Mix chicken stock and tomato paste together and pour over beans. (The contents of the pot won't be covered with liquid at this stage.) Season with salt and pepper, cover and simmer over a low heat for 4 hours. If liquid level remains below the beans after 1 hour, top it up with hot water to just cover. Give the pot a stir about every 45 minutes or so.

Stir and season to taste. Sprinkle remaining oregano into the pot just before serving.

Serves 6

Majorcan chicken

2 tablespoons olive oil
30 g (1 oz) butter
1.5 kg (3 lb 5 oz) chicken pieces
1 orange
1 red onion, thinly sliced
2 garlic cloves, chopped
185 ml (6 fl oz/³/₄ cup) chicken stock
125 ml (4 fl oz/¹/₂ cup) white wine
1 tablespoon plain (all-purpose) flour
1 red capsicum (pepper), quartered
12 stuffed green olives
15 g (¹/₂ oz) chopped parsley

Preheat the oven to 180°C (350°F/ Gas 4). Heat the oil and butter in a large pan. Brown chicken in batches over high heat and then transfer to a flameproof casserole dish.

Cut two large strips of rind from the orange and set aside. Remove the pith from the orange, then slice the orange into thin rounds. Set aside.

Cook onion and garlic in the pan for about 3 minutes over medium heat. Combine the stock and the wine. Stir flour into pan, then slowly add the stock and the wine and stir until mixture comes to the boil. Add the orange rind, then pour over chicken. Cover and bake for 1 hour.

Meanwhile, grill (broil) the capsicum, skin-side up, for 8 minutes, or until black and blistered. Place in a plastic bag, seal and allow to cool. Peel away the skin and cut the flesh into strips.

Remove chicken from dish; cover and keep warm. Bring sauce to the boil on the stovetop. Boil for 5 minutes. Add capsicum strips, orange slices, olives and parsley. To serve, remove orange rind, season to taste and then spoon sauce over the chicken.

Serves 4

Cassoulet

400 g (14 oz) dried haricot beans
bouquet garni
½ large onion, cut into quarters
2 garlic cloves, crushed
225 g (8 oz) salt pork or unsmoked
   bacon, cut into cubes
15 g (½ oz) clarified butter
400 g (14 oz) lamb shoulder
350 g (12 oz) boiling sausages
   (saucisses à cuire)
1 celery stalk, sliced
4 pieces duck confit or 4 pieces
   roasted duck
6 large tomatoes
180 g (6½ oz) Toulouse sausage
4 baguette slices, made into crumbs

Put beans in a bowl and cover with cold water. Soak overnight, then drain and rinse. Put the beans in a large saucepan with the bouquet garni, onion, garlic and the salt pork. Add 2–3 litres of cold water, bring to the boil and then simmer for 1 hour.

Heat butter in a frying pan. Cut lamb into eight pieces and brown in butter. Add lamb, boiling sausage, celery and duck confit to top of beans and push into liquid. Score a cross in the top of tomatoes, plunge into boiling water for 20 seconds, then peel skin away from cross. Chop and add to the cassoulet. Push into liquid and cook for an hour. Brown Toulouse sausage in frying pan, add to cassoulet and cook for 30 minutes. Preheat oven to 160°C (315°F/Gas 2–3).

Discard bouquet garni. Strain liquid into saucepan and boil over moderate heat until it is reduced by two-thirds. Remove all meat from saucepan and slice sausages and pull the duck meat from bones. Layer meat and beans, alternately, in a casserole dish. Pour in liquid, to come no higher than top of the beans. Sprinkle with breadcrumbs and then bake for 40 minutes. Every 10 minutes, break breadcrumb crust with spoon to let some liquid through.

Serves 6

Turkey osso buco

3 red capsicums (pepper)
2.1 kg (4 lb 8 oz) frozen turkey
 hindquarters (legs with thighs),
 chopped
seasoned plain (all-purpose) flour
60 ml (2 fl oz/¼ cup) olive oil
60 g (2¼ oz) butter
185 ml (6 fl oz/¾ cup) chicken stock
¼ teaspoon dried chilli flakes
4 fresh sage leaves, chopped, or
 ½ teaspoon dried sage
2 garlic cloves, crushed
1 teaspoon finely grated lemon rind
150 g (5½ oz) sliced pancetta, or
 thinly sliced bacon
1 rosemary sprig
2 tablespoons chopped flat-leaf
 (Italian) parsley

Preheat grill (broiler) to high. Cut the capsicums in half, then remove the seeds and membranes. Place the capsicum halves skin-side up under grill and cook for 5–8 minutes, or until skin blackens and blisters. Transfer to a plastic bag, seal and allow to cool, then peel away blackened skin. Cut flesh into thick slices.

Thaw turkey pieces in refrigerator. When thawed, pat with paper, then coat in the seasoned flour.

Heat the oil and the butter in a large saucepan. Brown the turkey pieces in batches over medium–high heat, then drain pan of excess oil. Pour chicken stock into pan and stir well, scraping the base and side of the pan to mix in all the pan juices. Add the chilli flakes, sage, garlic and the lemon rind, and cook, stirring, for 1 minute.

Return all turkey pieces to pan. Cover with grilled capsicum slices, then layer pancetta over top. Add the rosemary sprig, cover pan and cook over low heat for 1 hour, or until the turkey is succulent, yet not falling off the bone. Discard rosemary sprig and transfer the cooked turkey to a plate. Cover and keep warm. Stir in parsley, then spoon sauce over turkey to serve.

Serves 4–6

Abbacchio (Roman lamb)

60 ml (2 fl oz/¼ cup) olive oil
1 kg (2 lb 4 oz) spring lamb, cut into
  2 cm (¾ inch) cubes
2 garlic cloves, crushed
6 sage leaves
1 sprig rosemary
1 tablespoon flour
125 ml (4 fl oz/½ cup) white wine
  vinegar
6 anchovy fillets

Heat the oil in a heavy-based frying pan and cook the meat in batches over medium heat for 3–4 minutes, until browned on all sides.

Return all meat to the pan and add garlic, sage and rosemary. Season with salt and pepper, combine well and cook for 1 minute.

Dust meat with the flour using a fine sieve, then cook for another minute. Add the vinegar and simmer for 30 seconds, add 250 ml (9 fl oz/ 1 cup) water. Bring to a simmer, then lower the heat and cover, leaving the lid partially askew. Cook for around 50–60 minutes, or until the meat is tender, stirring occasionally and adding more water if necessary.

When lamb is almost cooked, mash anchovies in a mortar and pestle with 1 tablespoon of cooking liquid, until a paste is formed. Add to the lamb and then cook, uncovered, for another 2 minutes.

Serves 4–6

Veal goulash

500 g (1 lb) veal, cut into 2.5 cm (1 in)
 pieces
2 tablespoons plain (all-purpose) flour
2 tablespoons olive oil
2 onions, thinly sliced
2 garlic cloves, finely chopped
1 tablespoon sweet Hungarian
 paprika
1 teaspoon ground cumin
440 g (14 oz) tinned diced tomatoes
2 carrots, sliced
1/2 red capsicum (pepper), chopped
1/2 green capsicum (pepper), chopped
250 ml (9 fl oz/1 cup) beef stock
125 ml (4 fl oz/1/2 cup) red wine
125 g (41/2 oz/1/2 cup) sour cream
chopped parsley, to garnish

Put the veal and flour in a plastic bag and shake to coat the veal with flour. Shake off any excess. Heat 1 tablespoon of the oil in a deep heavy-based saucepan over medium heat. Brown the meat well in batches, then remove the meat and set aside.

Add remaining oil to the pan. Cook the onion, garlic, paprika and cumin for 5 minutes, stirring frequently. Return meat and any juices to the pan with the tomato, carrot and capsicum. Cover and cook for 10 minutes.

Add the stock and wine, and season with salt and pepper. Stir well, then cover and simmer over very low heat for 1 1/2 hours. Stir in half of the sour cream, then season with salt and pepper if needed and serve garnished with parsley and the remaining sour cream. Delicious served with buttered boiled small potatoes or noodles.

Serves 4

Beef provencale

1.5 kg (3 lb) chuck steak, cut into
3 cm (1 1/4 in) cubes
2 tablespoons olive oil
1 small onion, sliced
375 ml (12 fl oz/1 1/2 cups) red wine
2 tablespoons chopped flat-leaf
(Italian) parsley
1 tablespoon chopped rosemary
1 tablespoon chopped thyme
2 fresh bay leaves
250 g (8 oz) speck, rind removed, cut
into 1 x 2 cm (1/2 x 3/4 in) pieces
400 g (14 oz) tinned crushed
tomatoes
250 ml (9 fl oz/1 cup) beef stock
500 g (1 lb 2 oz) baby carrots
45 g (1 1/2 oz/1/3 cup) pitted niçoise
olives

In a bowl, combine cubed beef with
1 tablespoon of the oil, onion, 250 ml
(9 fl oz/1 cup) of wine and half of the
herbs. Cover with plastic wrap and
refrigerate overnight.

Drain beef, reserving the marinade.
Heat the remaining oil in a large
heavy-based saucepan and brown
beef and onion in batches. Remove
from the pan.

Add speck to saucepan and cook for
3–5 minutes, until crisp. Return beef
to pan with the remaining wine and
marinade and cook, scraping the
residue from the base of the pan for
2 minutes, or until wine has slightly
reduced. Add the tomato and stock
and bring the boil. Reduce the heat
and add the remaining herbs. Season
well, cover and simmer for 1 1/2 hours.

Add the carrots and olives to the
saucepan and cook, uncovered, for
another 30 minutes, or until the meat
and the carrots are tender. Before
serving, check the seasoning and
adjust if necessary.

Serves 6

Chicken stew with white beans and zucchini

1 tablespoon olive oil
8 boneless, skinless chicken thighs
1 onion, halved and thinly sliced
4 garlic cloves, finely chopped
3 tablespoons dry white wine
250 ml (9 fl oz/1 cup) chicken stock
1 tablespoon finely chopped rosemary
1 teaspoon grated lemon zest
1 bay leaf
800 g (1 lb 12 oz) tinned cannellini
  beans, drained and rinsed
3 zucchini (courgettes), halved
  lengthways, cut on the diagonal

Heat oil in a large ovenproof casserole dish. Add the chicken in batches, and cook for 4 minutes on each side, or until browned. Remove.

Add the onion to the dish and cook for 5 minutes, or until soft. Add the garlic and cook for 1 minute, or until fragrant, then add the wine and chicken stock and bring to the boil, scraping the bottom of the pan to remove any sediment.

Return the chicken and any juices to the pan along with the rosemary, lemon zest and bay leaf. Reduce the heat and simmer, covered, for 40 minutes, or until the chicken is tender. Stir in the cannellini beans and zucchini and cook for 5 minutes more, or until the zucchini is tender.

Serves 4

Spicy lamb casserole

3 tablespoons olive oil
1.25 kg (2 lb 12 oz) lamb leg or
   shoulder, cut into 4 cm (1½ in)
   cubes
1 small onion, finely chopped
1 celery stalk, finely chopped
3 garlic cloves, crushed
125 ml (4 fl oz/½ cup) dry Marsala
¾ teaspoon chilli flakes
1 tablespoon crushed juniper berries
2 tablespoons tomato paste
   (concentrated purée)
250 ml (9 fl oz/1 cup) chicken stock
1 rosemary sprig
12 small onions, such as cipolline or
   pearl onions
2 potatoes, cut into cubes
2 tablespoons finely chopped parsley

Preheat the oven to 180°C (350°F/ Gas 4). Heat the olive oil in a large casserole. Add the lamb in batches, season with salt and pepper and brown lightly over high heat. Remove each batch from the casserole as it browns. Once all the lamb is browned and has been removed from the casserole, add the onion, celery and garlic, reduce the heat and cook for 4–5 minutes until softened.

Return lamb to the casserole. Pour in the Marsala and cook over high heat until it is dark brown and reduced by half. Add the chilli flakes and juniper berries and cook, stirring, for about 10–15 seconds. Add tomato paste, chicken stock, rosemary and 250 ml (9 fl oz/1 cup) water, or enough water to just cover.

Cover casserole with a lid and bake in the oven for 45 minutes. Add the onions and the potato and cook for another 45 minutes. Stir the parsley through just before serving.

Serves 4

Mediterranean chicken

8 chicken thigh cutlets
2 tablespoons olive oil
150 g (5½ oz) French shallots
4 garlic cloves
125 ml (4 fl oz/½ cup) white wine
425 g (14 oz) tinned chopped
    tomatoes
12 Kalamata olives
1 tablespoon red wine vinegar
2 teaspoons tomato paste
    (concentrated purée)
1 tablespoon fresh oregano leaves
1 tablespoon chopped basil
1 teaspoon sugar
4 slices prosciutto
1 teaspoon grated lemon zest
30 g (1 oz/½ cup) chopped parsley
1 tablespoon capers, rinsed

Preheat the oven to 180°C (350°F/
Gas 4). Remove the skin and fat from
the chicken thighs. Heat half the oil in
a large pan and brown chicken over
high heat for 3–4 minutes on each
side. Arrange the chicken in a large
flameproof casserole dish.

Heat remaining oil in the same pan.
Add shallots and garlic and cook over
medium heat for 4 minutes, or until
soft but not brown. Add the wine and
bring to the boil.

Add the tomatoes, olives, vinegar,
tomato paste, oregano, basil and
sugar. Season with salt and black
pepper. Boil, stirring, for 2 minutes,
then pour over chicken and cover
with a lid. Bake for 45 minutes, or
until the chicken is tender.

Meanwhile, place the prosciutto in a
single layer in a frying pan. Dry-fry for
3 minutes, or until crisp, turning once.
Break into large chunks and set aside.

Arrange chicken on a serving dish,
cover and keep warm. Transfer the
casserole to the stove top and boil
pan juices for 5 minutes. Spoon the
juices over chicken and sprinkle with
the lemon zest, parsley and capers.
Top with the prosciutto.

Serves 4

Pork noisettes with prunes

8 pork noisettes or 2 x 400 g (14 oz)
  pork fillets
16 prunes, pitted
1 tablespoon oil
45 g (1½ oz) butter
1 onion, finely chopped
155 ml (5 fl oz) white wine
280 ml (10 fl oz) chicken or brown
  stock
1 bay leaf
2 thyme sprigs
250 ml (9 fl oz/1 cup) thick cream

Trim any excess fat from pork, making sure you get rid of any membrane. If you are using pork fillet, cut each fillet into four diagonal slices. Put prunes in a small saucepan, cover with cold water and bring to the boil. Reduce the heat and simmer the prunes for 5 minutes. Drain well.

Heat the oil in a large heavy-based frying pan and add half the butter. When butter starts foaming, add the pork, in batches if required, and sauté on both sides until cooked. Transfer to a warm plate and keep warm.

Pour off the excess fat from the pan. Melt remaining butter, add the onion and cook over low heat until softened but not browned. Add the wine, bring to the boil and simmer for 2 minutes. Add the stock, bay leaf and the thyme and bring to the boil. Reduce the heat and simmer for 10 minutes or until reduced by half.

Strain the stock into a bowl and rinse the frying pan. Return stock to pan, add cream and prunes and simmer for 8 minutes, or until sauce thickens slightly. Tip pork back into the pan and simmer until heated through.

Serves 4

Duck in red wine

4 duck Marylands (leg quarters)
4 duck breasts
3 tablespoons butter
2 onions, finely chopped
2 carrots, cubed
2 celery stalks, cubed
120 g (4½ oz) prosciutto, in thin strips
750 ml (1 bottle) Barolo, or other dry
  red wine
2 bay leaves
4 tablespoons Cognac

Prick the duck pieces all over. Melt 2 tablespoons of butter in a large flameproof casserole dish or stockpot and fry the duck in batches over a medium heat, skin-side-down. When they have given up a good amount of fat and turned light golden brown, remove from the pot. Pour off all but 2 tablespoons of the fat.

Preheat oven to 160°C (315°F/Gas 2–3). Add onions, carrots, celery and prosciutto to the pot and cook over a low heat for about 8–10 minutes until golden. Add duck and season with salt and freshly ground black pepper. Add 250 ml (1 cup) of wine, increase the heat and boil until the wine has reduced by half. Add remaining wine and bay leaves and bring to the boil.

Cover pot and transfer to the oven. Bake for 2 hours, or until tender. Transfer the duck pieces to a serving platter, cover with foil and keep warm. Put the pot over a high heat and bring to the boil. Add remaining butter and Cognac and boil until thickened. Taste for seasoning. Spoon over the duck and serve at once.

Serves 6–8

Navarin à la Printanière

1 kg (2 lb 4 oz) lean lamb shoulder
30 g (1 oz) butter
1 onion, chopped
1 garlic clove, crushed
1 tablespoon plain (all-purpose) flour
500 ml (17 fl oz/2 cups) brown stock
bouquet garni
18 baby carrots
8 large-bulb spring onions (scallions)
200 g (7 oz) baby turnips
175 g (6 oz) small potatoes
150 g (5½ oz) peas, fresh or frozen

Trim the lamb of any fat and sinew and then cut it into bite-sized pieces. Heat the butter over high heat in a large casserole. Brown the lamb in two or three batches, then remove from the casserole.

Add the onion to the casserole and cook, stirring, for 3 minutes or until softened but not browned. Add the garlic and cook for a further minute or until aromatic.

Return meat and any juices to the casserole and sprinkle with the flour. Stir over high heat until meat is well coated and liquid is bubbling, then gradually stir in the stock. Add the bouquet garni and bring to the boil. Reduce the heat to low, cover the casserole and cook for 1¼ hours.

Trim the carrots, leaving a little bit of green stalk, and do the same with the spring onions and baby turnips. Cut the potatoes in half if they are large.

Add vegetables to the casserole dish, bring to the boil and simmer, covered, for 15 minutes or until vegetables are tender. (If you are using frozen peas, add them right at the end so they just heat through.) Season before serving.

Serves 6

Kidneys turbigo

8 lamb kidneys
60 g (2¼ oz) butter
8 chipolata sausages
12 small pickling or pearl onions or
  shallots
125 g (4½ oz) button mushrooms,
  sliced
1 tablespoon plain (all-purpose) flour
2 tablespoons dry sherry
2 teaspoons tomato purée
250 ml (9 fl oz/1 cup) beef stock
2 tablespoons finely chopped parsley

Croutes
oil, for brushing
2 garlic cloves, crushed
12 slices baguette, cut on an angle

Trim, halve and cut white membrane from the kidneys. Heat half the butter in a frying pan and cook kidneys for 2 minutes. Remove to a plate. Add the chipolatas to frying pan and cook for 2 minutes until browned all over. Remove chipolatas to a plate. Cut in half on the diagonal.

Lower heat and add remaining butter to frying pan. Cook the onions and the mushrooms, stirring, for 5 minutes until soft. Mix together the flour and sherry to make a smooth paste. Add the tomato purée and stock and mix until smooth.

Remove the frying pan from the heat and stir in stock mixture. Return to the heat and stir until boiling. Season well. Return kidneys and chipolatas to sauce. Lower heat, cover the pan and simmer for 25 minutes, until cooked.

Meanwhile, to make croutes, preheat the oven to 180°C (350°F/Gas 4). Mix together oil and garlic and brush over bread slices. Place on a baking tray and bake for 3–4 minutes. Turn over and bake for a further 3 minutes until golden brown. Sprinkle kidneys with parsley and serve with the croutes on one side.

Serves 4

Braised lamb shanks with haricot beans

400 g (14 oz) dried haricot beans
4 tablespoons oil
4 lamb shanks, trimmed
2 tablespoons butter
2 garlic cloves, crushed
2 brown onions, finely chopped
1½ tablespoons thyme leaves
2 tablespoons tomato paste
   (concentrated purée)
800 g (1 lb 2 oz) tinned crushed
   tomatoes
1 tablespoon paprika
1 dried jalapeño chilli, roughly
   chopped
30 g (1 oz) roughly chopped flat-leaf
   (Italian) parsley

Put the haricot beans in a bowl, cover well with water and soak overnight.

Heat 3 tablespoons of the oil in a large heavy-based frying pan over medium heat and brown the shanks on all sides. Remove and set aside. Drain the fat from the pan.

Heat the butter and remaining oil in the pan and cook the garlic and onion over medium heat for 3–4 minutes, or until softened. Add the thyme, tomato paste, tomato and paprika and then simmer for 5 minutes. Add the lamb shanks and 500 ml (17 fl oz/2 cups) hot water. Season well and bring to the boil. Cover pan, reduce the heat and simmer gently for 30 minutes.

Drain beans and add to the pan with the jalapeño chilli and another 500 ml (17 fl oz/2 cups) of hot water. Bring to the boil again, cover and simmer for another 1–1½ hours or until both the beans and meat are tender, adding more water, 125 ml (4 fl oz/½ cup) at a time, if necessary. Check seasoning and stir in half the parsley. Serve hot sprinkled with the remaining parsley.

Serves 4

Veal, lemon and caper stew

1 tablespoon olive oil
50 g (1³/₄ oz) butter
1 kg (2 lb 4 oz) stewing veal, cut into
  4 cm (1¹/₂ in) chunks
300 g (10¹/₂ oz) French shallots
  (eschalots)
3 leeks, white part only, cut into large
  cubes
2 garlic cloves, crushed
1 tablespoon plain (all-purpose) flour
500 ml (17 fl oz/2 cups) chicken stock
1 teaspoon grated lemon zest
4 tablespoons lemon juice
2 bay leaves
2 tablespoons capers, drained and
  well rinsed

Preheat oven to 180°C (350°F/Gas 4). Heat oil and half the butter in a large, heavy-based saucepan. Brown veal in batches over medium–high heat and transfer to a large casserole dish.

Blanch the shallots in boiling water for 30 seconds, then peel and add to the saucepan with the leeks. Gently cook for 5 minutes, or until soft and golden. Add the garlic, cook for 1 minute, then transfer to the casserole dish.

Melt the remaining butter in the pan, add flour and cook for 30 seconds. Remove from the heat, add the stock and stir until combined. Return to the heat and cook, stirring, until the sauce begins to bubble.

Pour the sauce into the casserole dish and stir in the lemon zest, lemon juice and bay leaves. Cover and bake for 1–1¹/₂ hours, or until the veal is tender. During the last 20 minutes of cooking, remove the lid to allow the sauces to reduce a little. Stir in the capers and season before serving.

Serves 6

Beef goulash

1 kg (2 lb 4 oz) casserole beef (chuck or blade), cut into chunks
50 g (1¾ oz) plain (all-purpose) flour
1½ tablespoons vegetable oil
1 red onion, cut into wedges
2 garlic cloves, chopped
800 g (1 lb 12 oz) tinned chopped tomatoes
250 ml (9 fl oz/1 cup) beef stock
1 tablespoon tomato paste (concentrated purée)
1½ tablespoons Hungarian sweet paprika
2 bay leaves
2 boiling potatoes, cut into 1.5 cm (⅝ in) cubes
3 teaspoons oregano, chopped

Coat beef in flour and shake away any excess. Heat oil in a heavy-based saucepan over high heat. Cook beef in three batches for 2 minutes, or until browned. Add the onion and garlic and cook, stirring, for 2 minutes, or until slightly soft.

Return beef to the saucepan. Add the chopped tomatoes, beef stock, tomato paste, sweet paprika and bay leaves. Reduce the heat to medium and simmer, covered, for 30 minutes, stirring occasionally. Add the potato, and simmer, covered, for a further 20 minutes, or until beef and potato are tender. Remove the lid from the saucepan, and simmer for 5 minutes, or until slightly thick. Stir in oregano and season to taste.

Serves 4

Italian sausage and chickpea stew

2 large red capsicums (peppers)
1 tablespoon olive oil
2 large red onions, cut into thick
  wedges
2 garlic cloves, finely chopped
600 g (1 lb 5 oz) Italian-style thin pork
  sausages
300 g (10½ oz) tinned chickpeas,
  drained
150 g (5½ oz) flat mushrooms, thickly
  sliced
125 ml (4 fl oz/½ cup) dry white wine
2 bay leaves
2 teaspoons chopped rosemary
400 g (14 oz) tinned diced tomatoes

Cut the capsicums into large pieces, removing the seeds and membrane. Place skin-side up, under a hot grill (broiler) until the skin blackens and blisters. Allow to cool in a plastic bag. Peel away the skin, and slice diagonally into thick strips.

Meanwhile, heat the oil in a large non-stick frying pan. Add the onion and garlic, and stir over medium heat for 6 minutes, or until the onion is soft and browned. Remove onion from the pan and set aside. Add the sausages to the pan. Cook over medium heat, turning occasionally, for 8 minutes, or until sausages are browned. Remove the sausages from the pan and slice diagonally into 3 cm (1¼ in) pieces.

Combine the capsicum slices, onion, sausage pieces, the chickpeas and the mushrooms in the pan, and cook over medium–high heat.

Add wine, bay leaves and rosemary to the pan. Bring to the boil, then reduce the heat to low and simmer for about 3 minutes. Stir in tomato and simmer for 20 minutes, or until the sauce has thickened slightly. Remove bay leaves and season.

Serves 4

Osso buco with tomatoes

10 pieces veal shank, about 4 cm
  (1½ in) thick
plain (all-purpose) flour, seasoned with
  salt and pepper
60 ml (2¼ oz/¼ cup) olive oil
60 g (2¼ oz) butter
1 garlic clove
1 small carrot, finely chopped
1 large onion, finely chopped
½ celery stalk, finely chopped
250 ml (9 fl oz/1 cup) dry white wine
375 ml (13 fl oz/1½ cups) veal or
  chicken stock
400 g (14 oz) tinned chopped
  tomatoes
bouquet garni

Tie each piece of veal shank around its girth to secure the flesh, then dust with the seasoned flour. Heat the oil, butter and garlic in a heavy saucepan. Put shanks in the saucepan and cook for 12–15 minutes until well browned. Remove shanks from the saucepan and set aside. Discard the garlic.

Add the carrot, onion and celery to the saucepan and then cook over moderate heat for 5–6 minutes, without browning. Increase the heat to high, add the wine and cook for 2–3 minutes. Add stock, tomatoes and bouquet garni. Season with salt and pepper.

Return veal shanks to the saucepan, standing them up in a single layer. Cover the pan, reduce the heat and simmer for 1 hour, or until the meat is tender and you can cut it with a fork.

If you prefer a thicker sauce, remove the veal shanks and then increase the heat. Boil the sauce until reduced and thickened, then return the veal to the saucepan. Discard the bouquet garni, and taste for salt and pepper.

Serves 4

Creamy tomato and chicken stew

4 bacon slices
2 tablespoons oil
50 g (1³/₄ oz) butter
300 g (10½ oz) small button
  mushrooms, halved
1.5 kg (3 lb 5 oz) chicken pieces
2 onions, chopped
2 garlic cloves, crushed
400 g (14 oz) tinned tomatoes
250 ml (9 fl oz/1 cup) chicken stock
250 ml (9 fl oz/1 cup) cream
2 tablespoons chopped parsley
2 tablespoons lemon thyme leaves

Chop the bacon into large pieces. Place a large, heavy-based saucepan over medium heat. Brown the bacon, stirring, then remove and set aside on paper towels.

Heat half the oil and one-third of the butter in the saucepan until foaming, then add mushrooms and cook until they are softened and golden brown. Remove mushrooms from the pan with a slotted spoon.

Add the remaining oil to the pan with a little more butter. When the oil is hot, brown chicken pieces in batches over high heat until the skin is golden all over and a little crisp. Remove the chicken pieces from pan and drain on paper towels.

Heat the remaining butter in the pan. Add the onion and garlic, and cook over medium–high heat for about 3 minutes, or until softened. Pour in the tomatoes, stock and cream. Return the bacon, mushrooms and chicken pieces to the pan, and simmer over medium–low heat for 25 minutes. Stir in the parsley and thyme, season with salt and freshly ground pepper, and simmer for another 5 minutes before serving.

Serves 4–6

Beef and peppercorn stew

1 kg (2 lb) chuck steak, cut into 3 cm
(1 1/4 in) cubes
2 teaspoons cracked black
peppercorns
40 g (1 1/2 oz) butter
2 tablespoons oil
1 large onion, thinly sliced
2 garlic cloves, sliced
1 1/2 tablespoons plain (all-purpose)
flour
2 tablespoons brandy
750 ml (26 fl oz/3 cups) beef stock
1 tablespoon Worcestershire sauce
2 teaspoons Dijon mustard
500 g (1 lb 2 oz) baby new potatoes
60 ml (2 fl oz/1/4 cup) cream
2 tablespoons chopped parsley

Toss the steak in the peppercorns. Heat half the butter and half the oil in a large heavy-based saucepan. Brown half the steak over high heat, then remove and set aside. Heat the remaining butter and oil, and brown the remaining steak. Remove from the pan and set aside.

Add onion and garlic to the pan and cook, stirring, until onion is golden. Add the flour and stir until browned. Remove from the heat.

Combine the brandy, the beef stock, Worcestershire sauce and mustard, and gradually stir into onion mixture. Return to the heat, add the steak and any juices, then simmer, covered, for 1 1/4 hours.

Add potatoes and simmer, uncovered, for a further 30 minutes, or until meat and potatoes are tender. Stir in cream and parsley, and season to taste with salt and freshly ground pepper.

Serves 4

Moghul-style lamb

6 garlic cloves, roughly chopped
4 cm (1½ in) piece fresh ginger,
  roughly chopped
50 g (1¾ oz) blanched almonds
2 onions, thinly sliced
850 g (1 lb 14 oz) boneless leg or
  shoulder of lamb, cut into cubes
2 teaspoons coriander seeds
40 g (1½ oz) ghee
7 cardamom pods
5 cloves
1 cinnamon stick
1 teaspoon salt
300 ml (10½ fl oz) cream
½ teaspoon cayenne pepper
½ teaspoon garam masala
flaked almonds, toasted

Blend garlic, ginger, almonds and
50 g (1¾ oz) of the onion in a blender
or food processor. If you don't have a
blender, finely chop with a knife or
grind together with a mortar and
pestle. Add a little water, if necessary,
to make a smooth paste, then put
in a bowl with lamb and mix to coat
the meat. Cover and marinate in the
fridge for 2 hours, or overnight.

Put a small frying pan over a low heat
and dry-roast coriander seeds until
aromatic, then grind to a fine powder
using a spice grinder or mortar and
pestle. Heat ghee in a casserole dish.
Add cardamom pods, cloves and
cinnamon stick, and, after a couple of
seconds, add remaining onion and fry
until soft and brown. Transfer onion to
a plate. Fry meat and marinade in pan
until it is dry and slightly brown. Add
150 ml (5 fl oz) of hot water to pan,
cover tightly and cook over low heat
for 30 minutes, stirring occasionally.

Add ground coriander, salt, cream,
cayenne pepper and onion to pan,
cover and simmer for 30 minutes,
or until lamb is tender. Stir to prevent
lamb from sticking to pan. Remove
cardamom pods, cinnamon stick and
the cloves, then stir in garam masala.
Sprinkle with flaked almonds.

Serves 4

Chicken in saffron stew

60 ml (2 fl oz/¼ cup) olive oil
50g (1¾ oz/⅓ cup) blanched
  almonds
1 thick slice bread, crusts removed,
  cut into pieces
½ teaspoon ground cinnamon
pinch of saffron threads
2 garlic cloves
2 tablespoons chopped flat-leaf
  (Italian) parsley
1.5 kg (3 lb 5 oz) chicken, cut into
  8 pieces and seasoned with salt
2 brown onions, finely chopped
125 ml (4 fl oz/½ cup) fino sherry
375 ml (13 fl oz/1½ cups) chicken
  stock
1 bay leaf
2 thyme sprigs
2 tablespoons lemon juice
2 egg yolks

Heat 1 tablespoon of the oil in a heavy-based flameproof casserole dish over medium–high heat. Add the almonds and bread and fry for 3 minutes, or until golden. Remove and drain on paper towel. When cooled slightly, put in a mortar and pestle or food processor, add the cinnamon, saffron, garlic and half the parsley, and grind or process to a coarse, crumbly consistency.

Heat the remaining oil in the casserole dish over medium heat and brown the chicken pieces for avround 5 minutes. Remove to a plate. Add the onion and then cook gently for about 5 minutes, or until softened.

Return chicken pieces to casserole dish with the sherry, stock, bay leaf and thyme and simmer, covered, over medium heat for 1 hour. Remove the chicken and cover to keep warm. Add almond paste to the dish and cook for 1 minute. Remove from the heat and whisk in lemon juice, egg yolks and remaining parsley. Return casserole dish to the stovetop and stir over very low heat until just thickened slightly. Season to taste, return chicken to the casserole and gently warm through before serving.

Serves 4

Chicken, artichoke and broad bean stew

155 g (5½ oz/1 cup) frozen broad
    beans
8 chicken thighs (skin removed,
    optional)
60 g (2¼ oz/½ cup) seasoned plain
    (all-purpose) flour
2 tablespoons oil
1 large red onion, cut into small
    wedges
125 ml (4 fl oz/½ cup) dry white wine
310 ml (10 fl oz/1¼ cups) chicken
    stock
2 teaspoons finely chopped rosemary
340 g (11 oz) marinated artichokes,
    well drained and quartered
800 g (1 lb 10 oz) potatoes, cut into
    large cubes
60 g (2¼ oz) butter

Remove the skins from the broad beans. Coat the chicken in the flour, shaking off the excess. Heat the oil in a saucepan or flameproof casserole dish, then brown the chicken in two batches on all sides over medium heat. Remove and drain.

Add the onion to the pan and cook for 3–4 minutes, or until soft but not brown. Increase the heat to high, pour in the wine and boil for 2 minutes, or until reduced to a syrup. Stir in 1 cup (250 ml/8 fl oz) of the stock and bring just to the boil, then return the chicken to the pan with the rosemary. Reduce the heat to low and simmer, covered, for 45 minutes.

Add artichokes to the pan, increase the heat to high and return to the boil. Reduce to a simmer and then cook, uncovered, for 10–15 minutes. Add the beans and cook for a further 5 minutes.

Meanwhile, cook the potato in a saucepan of boiling water for about 15–20 minutes, or until tender. Drain, then return to the pan. Add the butter and the remaining stock, and mash with a potato masher. Serve on the side of the stew.

Serves 4

Sausage and lentil stew

3 tablespoons olive oil
850 g (1 lb 14 oz) Italian sausages
1 onion, chopped
3 garlic cloves, thinly sliced
1½ tablespoons chopped rosemary
800 g (1 lb 12 oz) tinned chopped
  tomatoes
16 juniper berries, lightly crushed
pinch of grated nutmeg
1 bay leaf
1 dried chilli, crushed
185 ml (6 fl oz/¾ cup) red wine
95 g (3¼ oz/½ cup) green lentils

Heat the oil in a large saucepan and cook the sausages for 5–10 minutes, until browned. Remove the sausages from the pan and reduce the heat. Add the onion and garlic to the pan and cook gently until the onion is soft.

Stir in rosemary, then add tomatoes and cook gently until reduced to a thick sauce. Add juniper berries, bay leaf, nutmeg, chilli, wine and 410 ml (14 fl oz/1²/₃ cups) water. Bring to the boil, then add lentils and sausages. Give the stew a good stir, cover pan and simmer gently for 40 minutes, or until the lentils are soft. Stir a couple of times to prevent the lentils sticking to the base of the pan. Add more water if lentils are still not cooked.

Serves 4

Venison al forno with tomatoes and porcini

20 g (³/₄ oz) dried porcini mushrooms
750 g (1 lb 10 oz) venison, cut into
    3 cm (1¼ in) cubes
4 tablespoons extra virgin olive oil
1 onion, finely chopped
1 large celery stalk, finely chopped
1 large carrot, finely chopped
2 garlic cloves, finely chopped
2 sage sprigs, chopped
400 g (14 oz) tinned tomatoes
100 ml (3½ fl oz) red wine

Put the porcini in a bowl, cover with 200 ml hot water and leave to soak for 15 minutes. Preheat the oven to 150°C (300°F/Gas 3).

Heat the olive oil in a casserole, add the venison in batches and brown on both sides. Remove the meat from the casserole as it is browned.

Add the onion, celery and carrot to the casserole to make a soffritto and reduce the heat a little. Add the garlic and cook the vegetables for about 10 minutes, or until slightly soft and transparent. Drain the mushrooms, reserving the soaking liquid, and add them to the casserole with the sage. Stir briefly, then add the tomatoes, breaking them up with a spoon.

Add the wine and mushroom soaking liquid and cook, stirring every now and then, for another 10 minutes. Return the venison to the casserole, season and bring just to the boil.

Cover the casserole and cook in the oven for about 2 hours. After the first 30 minutes, check that the meat is cooking at a gentle simmer. When the meat is tender, set it aside for an hour, then reheat gently before serving.

Serves 4

Chicken in beer

350 ml (12 fl oz) bottle of beer
  (Spanish if possible)
1 tablespoon dijon mustard
1 teaspoon sweet paprika (pimentón)
2 brown onions, diced
2 garlic cloves, crushed
1.5 kg (2 lb 12 oz) chicken, cut into
  pieces
2 tablespoons olive oil
1 green capsicum (pepper), diced
400 g (14 oz) tinned chopped
  tomatoes
1 onion, extra, diced
1 garlic clove, extra, crushed

Combine beer, mustard, paprika, half the onion, half the garlic and a large pinch of salt in a large bowl. Add the chicken, toss until well coated and marinate overnight covered in plastic wrap (film) in the refrigerator.

Preheat oven to 180°C (350°F/Gas 4). Heat the olive oil in a large flameproof casserole dish over medium heat, add the capsicum and the remaining onion and garlic and cook for 10 minutes, or until softened.

Stir in the chicken, marinade and the tomato and season well. Cover and bake for 45–60 minutes, or until the chicken is tender.

Serves 4

Balti chicken

1 kg (2 lb 4 oz) boneless, skinless
   chicken thighs
80 ml (2½ fl oz/⅓ cup) oil
1 large red onion, finely chopped
4–5 garlic cloves, finely chopped
1 tablespoon grated fresh ginger
2 teaspoons ground cumin
2 teaspoons ground coriander
1 teaspoon ground turmeric
½ teaspoon chilli powder
425 g (15 oz) tinned chopped
   tomatoes
1 green capsicum (pepper), seeded
   and diced
1–2 small green chillies, seeded and
   finely chopped
4 tablespoons chopped coriander
   (cilantro)
2 spring onions (scallions), chopped,
   to garnish

Remove any excess fat or sinew from the chicken thighs and cut into four or five even-sized pieces.

Heat a large wok over high heat, add the oil and swirl to coat the side. Add the onion and stir-fry over medium heat for 5 minutes, or until softened but not browned. Add the garlic and ginger and stir-fry for 3 more minutes.

Add the spices, 1 teaspoon salt and 60 ml (2 fl oz/¼ cup) water. Increase the heat to high and stir-fry for 2 minutes, or until the mixture has thickened. Take care not to burn.

Add the tomato and 250 ml (9 fl oz/ 1 cup) water and cook, stirring often, for a further 10 minutes, or until the mixture is thick and pulpy and the oil comes to the surface.

Add the chicken to the pan, reduce the heat and simmer, stirring often, for 15 minutes. Add the capsicum and chilli and simmer for a further 25 minutes, or until chicken is tender. Add a little water if the mixture is too thick. Stir in the coriander and then garnish with the spring onion.

Serves 6

Chilli beef with capsicum, coriander and avocado

275 g (9¾ oz) red kidney beans
3 tablespoons olive oil
2 onions, chopped
2 fat garlic cloves, crushed
4 medium-hot green chillies,
  deseeded and finely chopped
110 g (4 oz) dark-gilled field
  mushrooms, chopped small
800 g (1 lb 12 oz) chuck steak, cubed
2 teaspoons ground cumin
½ teaspoon ground cinnamon
1 teaspoon caster (superfine) sugar
2 bay leaves
800 g (1 lb 12 oz) tinned chopped
  tomatoes
200 ml (7 fl oz) beef stock
1 red capsicum (pepper), diced
6 tablespoons coriander (cilantro)
  leaves
25 g (1 oz) dark, bitter chocolate
  (Mexican if possible), grated
1 firm, ripe avocado
½ red onion, chopped
250 g (9 oz) sour cream

Put the kidney beans in a bowl and cover with cold water. Leave to soak overnight, then drain and rinse. Heat 2 tablespoons of the oil in a large saucepan and add the onion. Cook gently for 10 minutes or until softened and translucent. Add garlic, chillies and mushrooms and continue to cook for 5 minutes, stirring now and then. Transfer onion mixture to a plate. Add remaining oil to the pan and, when very hot, brown the beef in batches.

Return the onion mixture to the pan to join the beef and add cumin, bay leaves, cinnamon, sugar, tomatoes, stock and beans. Stir together and bring to the boil. Reduce heat to low, cover and simmer gently for 1 hour. Add the capsicum and simmer for a further 30 minutes.

Stir in 4 tablespoons of coriander and all of the chocolate. Season to taste with salt and extra fresh chilli.

Chop avocado and mix with the red onion and remaining coriander leaves. Top each serving with a spoonful of the sour cream and a spoonful of the avocado mixture.

Serves 8

Chicken Marsala

60 ml (2 fl oz/¼ cup) olive oil
3 leeks, thinly sliced
1 teaspoon finely chopped rosemary
3 bay leaves, torn
1 kg (2 lb 4 oz) chicken pieces
seasoned plain (all-purpose) flour
1 large eggplant (aubergine), cut into
  cubes
2 zucchini (courgette), roughly
  chopped
125 ml (4 fl oz/½ cup) Marsala
300 ml (10½ fl oz) chicken stock
500 ml (16 fl oz/2 cups) tomato purée
200 g (7 oz) button mushrooms,
  halved

Heat the oil in a large, heavy-based saucepan. Fry leek, rosemary and bay leaves over low heat for 5 minutes, or until soft, stirring every now and then. Remove with a slotted spoon, leaving as much oil in the pan as possible.

Toss chicken pieces in the seasoned flour. Add the chicken to the pan and brown well in batches over medium heat. Return all the chicken to the pan along with the leek mixture.

Add the eggplant and zucchini, and cook, stirring, for 2–3 minutes, or until softened, turning the chicken. Add the Marsala and stock, and cook for 15 minutes over medium–high heat.

Add tomato purée and season well with salt and pepper. Bring to the boil, turning chicken pieces in the sauce. Reduce heat to a very gentle simmer, then cover and cook for 35 minutes. Add the mushrooms and then cook, uncovered, for 5 minutes.

Serves 4

Boeuf en daube

Marinade
2 cloves
1 onion, quartered
500 ml (17 fl oz/2 cups) red wine
2 strips orange zest
2 garlic cloves
½ celery stalk
2 bay leaves
a few parsley stalks

Daube
1.5 kg (3 lb 5 oz) beef topside, blade or rump
2 tablespoons oil
3 strips pork fat
1 pig's trotter or 225 g (8 oz) piece streaky bacon
700 ml (24 fl oz) beef stock

To make the marinade, push the cloves into a piece of onion and mix in a bowl with the remaining marinade ingredients. Cut the beef into pieces, season with salt and pepper, add to the marinade and leave overnight.

Heat oil in a saucepan. Lift the beef out of the marinade and pat dry, then brown in batches in the oil. Remove to a plate.

Strain the marinade through a sieve into a bowl and tip the contents of the sieve into the pan to brown. Remove from the pan. Add the marinade liquid to the pan and boil, stirring, for 30 seconds to deglaze the pan.

Put the pork fat in a large casserole dish, then add the pig's trotter, beef and marinade ingredients. Pour in the marinade liquid and stock. Bring to the boil, then cover, reduce the heat and simmer gently for 2–2½ hours.

Lift meat out of the casserole and transfer to a serving dish, cover and keep warm. Discard the garlic, onion, pork fat and pig's trotter. Pour liquid through a fine sieve, then return it to the casserole dish. Bring to the boil and boil until reduced by half. Pour the gravy over the meat.

Serves 6

Persian chicken

1.5 kg (3 lb) small chicken thighs
60 g (2¼ oz/½ cup) plain (all-
  purpose) flour
2 tablespoons olive oil
1 large onion, chopped
2 garlic cloves, chopped
½ teaspoon ground cinnamon
4 ripe tomatoes, chopped
6 fresh dates, stones removed, halved
2 tablespoons currants
500 ml (17 fl oz/2 cups) rich chicken
  stock
2 teaspoons finely grated lemon zest
80 g (2¾ oz/½ cup) almonds,
  toasted and roughly chopped
2 tablespoons chopped parsley

Coat chicken pieces with flour and shake off any excess. Heat oil in a large heavy-based pan over medium heat. Brown the chicken on all sides, turning regularly, and then remove from the pan. Drain any excess oil from the pan.

Add the onion, garlic and the ground cinnamon to pan and cook, stirring regularly, for 5 minutes, or until the onion is soft.

Add the tomato, dates, currants and stock, and bring to the boil. Return the chicken to the pan, cover with the sauce, reduce the heat and simmer, uncovered, for 30 minutes. Add the lemon rind and then season to taste. Bring back to the boil and boil for about 5 minutes, or until thickened. Sprinkle with almonds and parsley, and serve with buttered rice.

Serves 6

Valencian lamb and rice

100 g (3½ oz/½ cup) chickpeas
1 red onion
1 parsnip
1 celery stick
1 turnip
200 g (7 oz) diced lamb leg
1 pig's ear, about 150–200 g
    (5½–7 oz), salted if possible
100 g (3½ oz) minced (ground) pork
4 tablespoons fine fresh breadcrumbs
50 g (1¾ oz) jamón, finely chopped
1 egg
pinch of ground cinnamon
3 tablespoons chopped flat-leaf
    (Italian) parsley
1 morcilla or other blood sausage,
    about 200 g (7 oz)
1 white catalan sausage, butifarra or
    other mild pork sausage, about
    200 g (7 oz)
2 tablespoons olive oil
1 garlic clove, finely chopped
300 g (10½ oz/1⅓ cups) shortgrain
    rice

Soak the chickpeas in water for
3–4 hours and then drain. Meanwhile
chop onion, parsnip, celery and turnip
into 2 cm (¾ in) dice and set aside.
Bring 2 litres (70 fl oz/8 cups) of water
to the boil in a pot. Add diced lamb
and pig's ear. Bring water back to boil
then reduce to a simmer and cook for
30 minutes. Next, add diced onion,
chickpeas, parsnip, celery and turnip
and season. Simmer for 20 minutes.

Combine pork mince with cinnamon,
breadcrumbs, jamón, the egg, and
1 tablespoon of parsley. Season well.
Take heaped teaspoons of the mixture
and roll into balls. Add meatballs and
whole sausages to pot. Allow to come
back up to the simmer and cook for
10 more minutes or until meatballs
are cooked. Cover and turn off heat.

Preheat oven to 180°C (350°F/Gas 4).
Place a heavy based flameproof
casserole on stovetop over medium–
high heat. Add oil and chopped garlic
and cook, stirring for 2 minutes or
until garlic is lightly golden. Add rice
and stir for another minute. Stir in
600 ml (21 fl oz) of the cooking liquid
from the stew. Bring to boil, cover and
place in oven for 20 minutes or until
rice is cooked. Gently reheat stew
and serve rice, garnished with parsley.

Serves 4–6

Apricot chicken

6 chicken thigh cutlets
425 ml (14 fl oz) tinned apricot nectar
40 g (1½ oz) packet French onion
  soup mix
425 g (14 oz) tinned apricot halves in
  natural juice, drained
60 g (2¼ oz/¼ cup) sour cream

Preheat the oven to 180°C (350°F/ Gas 4). Remove skin from chicken thigh cutlets. Put the chicken in an ovenproof dish. Mix apricot nectar with the French onion soup mix until well combined, and pour over the chicken.

Bake, covered, for 50 minutes, then add the apricot halves and bake for a further 5 minutes. Stir in the sour cream just before serving. Delicious served with creamy mashed potato or rice to soak up the juices.

Serves 6

Oxtail stew

2 kg (4 lb 8 oz) oxtails, cut into 2 cm
   (³/₄ in) thick pieces
seasoned plain (all-purpose) flour, for
   dusting
80 ml (2½ fl oz/⅓ cup) olive oil
2 brown onions, chopped
1 leek, white part only, diced
2 carrots, diced
1 celery stalk, chopped
2 garlic cloves, crushed
400 g (14 oz) tinned chopped
   tomatoes
375 ml (13 fl oz/1½ cups) white wine
375 ml (13 fl oz/1½ cups) beef stock
1 teaspoon sweet paprika (pimentón)
1 bay leaf
2 tablespoons chopped thyme
2 tablespoons chopped flat-leaf
   (Italian) parsley

Preheat the oven to 150°C (300°F/
Gas 2). Coat oxtails with seasoned
flour. Heat 2 tablespoons of the oil
in a large, heavy-based flameproof
casserole dish over medium heat and
brown the oxtails in batches. Remove
to a plate.

Heat remaining oil in casserole dish
over medium heat, add the onion, the
leek, carrot, celery and the garlic and
then cook for 5 minutes, or until the
vegetables are softened.

Stir in tomato, wine, stock, paprika,
bay leaf and thyme and bring to the
boil. Add oxtails, making sure they
are covered in liquid (add extra water
if necessary), then cover and bake for
4–5 hours, depending on size of the
tails. The meat should easily fall away
from the bone when ready. Season to
taste and and serve garnished with
chopped parsley.

Serves 4–6

Seafood soups

Laksa lemak

115 g (4 oz) rice noodles
50 g (1³/₄ oz) unsalted macadamias
1 tablespoon oil
800 ml (28 fl oz) canned coconut milk
80 ml (2¹/₂ fl oz/¹/₃ cup) lime juice
115 g (4 oz) bean sprouts, trimmed
20 large raw prawns (shrimp), peeled
  and deveined
16 large scallops, cleaned
1 handful Vietnamese mint, shredded,
  a few leaves left whole to garnish
¹/₂ Lebanese (short) cucumber, peeled
  and thinly sliced

Paste
3 red chillies, seeded and chopped
2 lemongrass stems
a small knob fresh ginger, grated
4 red Asian shallots, peeled
3 teaspoons shrimp paste
3 teaspoons ground turmeric

Soak the noodles in boiling water for 10 minutes. Drain. To make the paste, put all the paste ingredients, plus 1 tablespoon of water, into a food processor and blend until smooth.

Alternatively, finely chop by hand and mix well. Put nuts in a saucepan and dry-roast over medium heat, shaking pan, until golden. Transfer to a plate.

Heat the oil in the same saucepan, add the prepared paste and cook over medium heat for 2 minutes. Stir in coconut milk, then gently simmer for 10 minutes, or until it thickens.

Roughly chop nuts. When coconut milk mixture is ready, add the lime juice and three quarters of the bean sprouts to pan. Season with the salt, bring back to a simmer, then add the prawns and the scallops and cook for about 5 minutes, or until the prawns have turned pink.

Add shredded mint and the noodles. Mix whole mint leaves with chopped nuts and cucumber. Ladle into 4 deep bowls, then sprinkle with the rest of the bean sprouts and mint and the cucumber mixture.

Serves 4

Seafood soup with alioli

1 tablespoon olive oil
1 carrot, finely diced
1 white onion, finely diced
1 leek, finely diced
3 garlic cloves, chopped
1 small red chilli, seeded and finely
  chopped
1 celery stalk, finely diced
2 large all-purpose potatoes, peeled
  and cut into 2 cm (³/₄ in) dice
500 g (1 lb 2 oz) skinless firm white
  fish fillets, cut into 2 cm (³/₄ in)
  cubes, reserving any bones
  and scraps
1 bay leaf
250 ml (9 fl oz/1 cup) white wine
30 ml (1 fl oz/1½ tablespoon) brandy
400 g (14 oz) tinned chopped
  tomatoes, drained
60 ml (2 fl oz/¼ cup) tomato paste
  (concentrated purée)
12 black mussels, bearded and
  scrubbed
8 raw king prawns (shrimp), peeled
  and deveined, tails intact
2 tablespoons lemon juice
2 tablespoons chopped flat-leaf
  (Italian) parsley

Heat the oil in a large saucepan over medium heat. Add carrot, onion, leek, garlic, chilli and celery and cook for 5 minutes. Add potato and 1.5 litres (52 fl oz/6 cups) of cold water. Bring to the boil, then reduce the heat and then simmer for 8 minutes, or until the potatoes are half cooked. Stir in the fish bones and scraps and bay leaf and simmer for 6–8 minutes, or until the potatoes are soft. Strain liquid and reserve. Remove the bones and bay leaf, and purée remaining potato and vegetable mixture with reserved liquid.

In a separate saucepan, combine the wine, brandy, chopped tomato and the tomato paste and bring to the boil. Add the mussels and cook, covered, for 3–5 minutes, or until opened. Remove from the pan, discarding any that remain closed.

Blend mussel-cooking liquid with the potato purée. Transfer to a large saucepan and bring to the boil. Add fish cubes and prawns, reduce heat and simmer for 8 minutes, or until all the seafood is cooked.

Stir in mussels and lemon juice and gently heat through. Season well and garnish with the parsley.

Serves 4–6

Creamy clam soup

1.75 kg (4 lb) clams, cleaned
800 ml–1 litre (28–35 fl oz) fish stock
50 g (1³/₄ oz) butter
1 onion, chopped
1 celery stalk, chopped
1 large carrot, chopped
1 large leek, sliced into rings
250 g (9 oz) swede (rutabaga), diced
1 bay leaf
70 g (2¹/₂ oz/heaped ¹/₃ cup) medium-
    or short-grain rice
200 ml (7 fl oz) cream
 3 tablespoons flat-leaf (Italian) parsley
    finely chopped

Put clams and 250 ml (9 fl oz/1 cup) water in a large saucepan. Bring to the boil, then reduce heat to medium and cover with a tight-fitting lid. Cook for 3– 4 minutes, or until shells open. Strain into a bowl. Add enough fish stock to make up to 1 litre (35 fl oz/ 4 cups). Discard any clams that are closed. Remove all but 8 of the clams from their shells.

Melt butter in a clean saucepan. Add the vegetables and then cook, covered, over medium heat for about 10 minutes, stirring occasionally. Add stock mixture and the bay leaf, bring to the boil, then reduce the heat and simmer for 10 minutes. Add the rice, return to the boil, cover and cook over medium heat for 15 minutes, or until rice and vegetables are tender. Remove from the heat and stir in the clam meat. Remove the bay leaf and allow mixture to cool for 10 minutes.

Purée the soup until smooth, then return to a clean saucepan. Stir in the cream, season and gently reheat. Divide among 4 bowls, and add the parsley and two reserved clams to each bowl.

Serves 4

Stuffed squid soup

280 g (10 oz) small squid
2 coriander (cilantro) roots, finely
   chopped
3–4 large garlic cloves, roughly
   chopped
280 g (10 oz) minced (ground) pork or
   chicken
¼ teaspoon salt
¼ teaspoon ground white pepper
2 litres (70 fl oz/8 cups) vegetable
   stock
2.5 cm (1 in) piece of ginger, sliced
4 tablespoons light soy sauce
1 tablespoon preserved radish, sliced
5 spring onions (scallions), slivered,
   to garnish
a few coriander (cilantro) leaves,
   to garnish
ground white pepper, for sprinkling

To clean each squid, grasp the squid body in one hand and pull away the head and tentacles from the body. Cut the head off the tentacles just above the eyes and discard the head. Clean out the body. Pull the skin off the squid and rinse well. Drain well.

Using a pestle and mortar, pound the garlic and the coriander roots into a paste. In a bowl, combine coriander paste with pork or chicken and salt and pepper. Spoon some mixture into a squid sac until two-thirds full. Squeeze the squid tube closed at the end. With a bamboo stick or sharp toothpick, prick several holes in the body of the squid. Place on a plate and repeat with the rest. Shape the remaining meat mixture into small balls about 1 cm (½ in) across.

Heat the stock to boiling point in a saucepan. Reduce heat to low and add the ginger, light soy sauce and preserved radish. Lower meatballs into the stock, then drop in stuffed squid and cook over a low heat for 4–5 minutes or until the meatballs and squid are cooked.

Garnish with coriander leaves and spring onions. Sprinkle with pepper.

Serves 4

Seafood laksa

1 kg (2 lb 4 oz) raw prawns (shrimp)
125 ml (4 fl oz/½ cup) oil
2–6 red chillies, seeded
1 onion, roughly chopped
3 garlic cloves, halved
2 cm (¾ in) piece fresh ginger or
  galangal, quartered
1 teaspoon ground turmeric
1 tablespoon ground coriander
3 lemongrass stems, white part only,
  chopped
1–2 teaspoons shrimp paste
600 ml (21 fl oz) coconut cream
2 teaspoons grated palm sugar
  (jaggery)
4 kaffir lime leaves
200 g (7 oz) packet fish balls
190 g (6¾ oz) packet fried bean curd
  pieces
250 g (9 oz) fresh thin egg noodles
250 g (9 oz) bean sprouts
1 large handful mint, chopped,
  to serve
1 handful coriander (cilantro) leaves,
  to serve

Peel and devein the prawns, keeping shells, heads and tails. To make the prawn stock, heat 2 tablespoons of toil in a heavy-based saucepan and add prawn shells, heads and tails. Stir until heads are bright orange, then add 1 litre (35 fl oz/4 cups) water. Bring to the boil, reduce heat and simmer for 15 minutes. Strain through a sieve, discarding shells.

Put chillies, onion, garlic, ginger (or galangal), turmeric, ground coriander, lemongrass and 60 ml (2 fl oz/¼ cup) of the stock in a food processor and process until chopped.

Heat remaining oil in a saucepan and add chilli mixture and shrimp paste. Stir over low heat for 3 minutes, or until fragrant. Pour in remaining stock and simmer for 10 minutes. Add palm sugar, coconut cream, makrut leaves and 2 teaspoons of salt. Simmer for 5 minutes. Add prawns and simmer for 2 minutes, until just pink. Remove and set aside. Add fish balls and bean curd and simmer until heated through. Boil water in a pan and cook noodles for 2 minutes. Drain and place in a bowl. Put the sprouts and prawns on noodles and pour soup over the top. Sprinkle with mint and coriander.

Serves 4–6

Crab bisque

1 kg (2 lb 4 oz) live crabs
50 g (1³/₄ oz) butter
½ carrot, finely chopped
½ onion, finely chopped
1 stalk celery, finely chopped
1 bay leaf
2 thyme sprigs
2 tablespoons tomato paste
  (concentrated purée)
2 tablespoons brandy
150 ml (5 fl oz) dry white wine
1 litre (35 fl oz/4 cups) fish stock
60 g (2¼ oz/⅓ cup) medium grain
  rice
60 ml (2 fl oz/¼ cup) thick
  (double/heavy) cream
¼ teaspoon cayenne pepper

Freeze crabs for 1–2 hours to immobilize them, then drop into boiling water and cook just until the shells turn red. Remove with tongs. Set aside until cool enough to handle.

Detach the claws and legs. Reserve 4 of the claws to use as a garnish. Crack any remaining claws and the legs, removing any meat and reserving the meat and shells separately. Snap off the flap on the underside of the body, then turn over and pull the top shell away from the bottom shell. Remove and discard the feathery gills and stomach sac and snap off the mouth. Pick the meat out of the shells, reserving meat and shells separately.

Heat the butter in a saucepan. Add the vegetables, bay leaf and thyme and cook over medium heat for 3 minutes. Add the reserved crab shells, the tomato paste, brandy and white wine and simmer for 2 minutes, or until reduced by half.

Add the stock and 500 ml (17 fl oz/ 2 cups) water and bring to the boil. Reduce the heat and simmer for 5 minutes. Remove the shells and finely crush them in a mortar and pestle. Return the crushed shells to the soup with the rice and the reserved crab meat. Bring to the boil, reduce the heat, cover and simmer for about 20 minutes, or until the rice is soft.

Immediately strain the bisque into a clean saucepan through a fine sieve lined with damp muslin, pressing down firmly on the solids to extract all the liquid. Add the cream and season with salt and cayenne pepper, then gently reheat. Ladle into warmed soup bowls and garnish with the crab claws.

Serves 4

Mediterranean fish soup

½ teaspoon saffron threads
2 teaspoons olive oil
2 large onions, thinly sliced
1 leek, chopped
4 garlic cloves, finely chopped
1 bay leaf, torn
½ teaspoon dried marjoram
1 teaspoon grated orange zest
2 tablespoons dry white wine
1 red capsicum (pepper), cut into
  bite-sized pieces
500 g (1 lb 2 oz) ripe tomatoes,
  chopped
125 ml (4 fl oz/½ cup) tomato
  passata (puréed tomatoes)
500 ml (17 fl oz/2 cups) fish stock
2 tablespoons tomato paste
  (concentrated purée)
2 teaspoons soft brown sugar
500 g (1 lb 2 oz) skinless and
  boneless fish fillets, trimmed and
  cut into bite-sized pieces
3 tablespoons chopped parsley
4 wholegrain bread rolls or slices

Soak the saffron threads in a bowl with 2 tablespoons of boiling water.

Heat the oil in a large saucepan over low heat. Add the onion, leek, garlic, bay leaf and marjoram. Cover and cook for 10 minutes, shaking the pan, until the onion is soft. Add the zest, wine, capsicum and tomato, cover and cook for 10 minutes.

Add the tomato passata, fish stock, tomato paste, sugar and saffron (with the liquid) to the pan. Stir well and bring to the boil, then reduce the heat to low and simmer, uncovered, for 15 minutes.

Add the fish to the soup, cover and cook for 8 minutes, or until tender. Add half the parsley, then season to taste with salt and freshly ground black pepper. Discard the bay leaf. Sprinkle the soup with the remaining parsley just before serving.

Warm bread, then serve with soup.

Serves 4

Prawn, scallop and noodle soup

4 dried shiitake mushrooms
100 g (3½ oz) dried soba (buckwheat) or somen noodles
10 g (¼ oz) sachet bonito-flavoured soup stock
80 g (2¾ oz) carrots, cut into thin batons
150 g (5½ oz) firm tofu, cut into cubes
16 raw prawns (shrimp), peeled and deveined, tails intact
8 scallops
2 spring onions (scallions), finely chopped
1 tablespoon mirin
shichimi togarashi (Japanese seven-spice seasoning mix), optional

Put mushrooms in a bowl and cover with 300 ml (10½ fl oz) of the boiling water. Place a saucer on top of the mushrooms to submerge them in the liquid, and then soak for 15 minutes. Meanwhile, bring a saucepan of water to the boil for the noodles. Cook the noodles until just tender, then drain. Return cooked noodles to pan and cover to keep warm.

In a saucepan, mix 1 litre (35 fl oz/ 4 cups) of water and stock. Drain the mushrooms and add the mushroom-soaking liquid to the pan. Chop the mushroom caps, discarding stalks.

Add mushrooms and carrot to pan and bring liquid to the boil. Reduce the heat to a simmer and cook for 5 minutes. Add tofu, prawns, spring onions, scallops and mirin to the pan. Cook at a gentle simmer for a further 3–4 minutes, or until prawns are pink and are cooked through and scallops are firm and opaque.

Meanwhile, pour hot water over the noodles and swish them around in water to separate and warm. Divide noodles between 4 large bowls and pour soup over, dividing the seafood equally. Serve, offering the shichimi togarashi to sprinkle over top.

Serves 4

Bouillabaisse

Rouille
1 small red capsicum (pepper)
1 slice white bread, crusts removed
1 red chilli
2 garlic cloves
1 egg yolk
4 tablespoons olive oil

Soup
18 mussels
1.5 kg (3 lb 5 oz) firm white fish fillets
  such as bass or snapper, skin on
2 tablespoons oil
1 fennel bulb, thinly sliced
1 onion, chopped
750 g (1 b 10 oz) ripe tomatoes
1.25 litres (44 fl oz/5 cups) fish stock
pinch saffron threads
1 bouquet garni
5 cm (2 in) piece orange zest

To make rouille, preheat grill (broiler). Cut capsicum in half, remove seeds and membrane and place, skin side up, under hot grill until skin blackens and blisters. Leave to cool before peeling away skin. Roughly chop.

Soak bread in 3 tablespoons of water, then squeeze dry. Put capsicum, chilli bread, garlic and egg yolk in a mortar and pestle and pound together. Add the oil in a thin stream, until rouille the has texture of mayonnaise. Cover and refrigerate. To make soup, scrub the mussels and pull out the hairy beards. Discard any broken mussels, or open ones that don't close when tapped on bench. Rinse. Cut the fish into small pieces. Cook the fennel and onion over medium heat for 5 minutes.

Score a cross in base of each tomato. Plunge them into boiling water for 20 seconds, drain and peel skin away from cross. Chop and add to pan. Stir in bouquet garni, stock, saffron and orange zest, bring to the boil and boil for 10 minutes. Remove the bouquet garni and push soup through a sieve. Return to pan, season and bring back to the boil. Reduce heat, add mussels and fish. Cook for about 5 minutes, or until mussels open. Discard any that don't. Serve with rouille and bread.

Serves 6

Cullen skink

600 g (1 lb 5 oz) smoked haddock,
(preferably Finnan haddock)
1.3 litres (45 fl oz) milk
25 g (1 oz) butter
100 g (3½ oz) smoked streaky bacon,
diced
1 large onion, chopped
500 g (1 lb 2 oz) waxy potatoes,
peeled and cut into small chunks
60 ml (2 fl oz/¼ cup) cream
3 tablespoons chives, chopped

Put haddock in a sauté pan or deep frying pan and pour milk over the top. Bring liquid to the boil, then reduce to a simmer, cover and poach gently for 10 minutes. When ready, fish should be flaky when tested with a knife.

Drain, reserving the milk. Flake the haddock into small pieces, discarding any skin and bones. Set aside.

Meanwhile, melt butter in a large saucepan and when foaming, add the bacon and onion. Cook on a medium–low heat for 10 minutes, or until the onion has softened.

Add the potatoes and the reserved milk. Bring to the boil and simmer, covered, for 15–20 minutes, or until the potatoes are cooked. Stir in the haddock and cream, season to taste with salt and pepper, and bring back to a gentle simmer. Sprinkle the chopped chives over the top.

Serves 4

Potato and anchovy chowder with garlic prawns

Garlic prawns
2 garlic cloves, chopped
1 small red chilli, seeded and
  chopped
2 tablespoons chopped flat-leaf
  (Italian) parsley
1 tablespoon olive oil
16 raw prawns (shrimp), peeled and
  deveined

1 tablespoon olive oil
3 bacon slices, fat trimmed, chopped
1 onion, chopped
2 celery stalks, chopped
2 garlic cloves, chopped
80 g (2¾ oz) tinned anchovies,
  drained
1 carrot, chopped
3 potatoes, roughly chopped
375 ml (13 fl oz/1½ cups) chicken
  stock or fish stock
250 ml (9 fl oz/1 cup) milk
125 ml (4 fl oz/½ cup) pouring cream
3 tablespoons finely chopped flat-leaf
  (Italian) parsley

To make garlic prawns, put garlic, chilli and parsley in a processor. Whizz for 15–20 seconds. With the motor running, add oil and whizz to form a rough paste. Transfer to a bowl, add prawns and toss to coat. Marinate for 30 minutes.

Heat oil in a heavy-based saucepan over medium–low heat. Add bacon, onion, celery and garlic and cook, stirring, for 2 minutes. Reduce heat, cover and simmer for 5 minutes.

Drain anchovies on paper towels and pat dry. Roughly chop and add to the bacon mixture. Add carrot and potato and stir. Cook for 2 minutes, then add stock and milk. Bring to the boil, then cover and cook for 15 minutes, or until vegetables are tender. Remove the saucepan from the heat. Using an immersion blender fitted with the chopping blade, whizz the soup for 20–30 seconds, or until smooth. Add cream and parsley, reserving some for garnishing. Season and keep warm.

Heat a frying pan over high heat and add the prawns and marinade. Cook, turning, for 2 minutes, or until prawns are cooked through. Place a pile of prawns in centre of bowl and ladle soup around. Sprinkle with parsley.

Serves 4

Bourride

Garlic croutons
½ baguette, day-old, sliced
3 tablespoons olive oil
1 garlic clove, halved

Aïoli
2 egg yolks
4 garlic cloves, crushed
4 teaspoons lemon juice
250 ml (9 fl oz/1 cup) olive oil

Stock
¼ teaspoon saffron threads
1 litre (35 fl oz/4 cups) dry white wine
1 leek, white part only, chopped
2 carrots, chopped
2 onions, chopped
2 orange zest long pieces
2 fennel seeds teaspoons
3 thyme sprigs
2.5 kg (5 lb 8 oz) firm white fish such
   as cod, perch or sole, filleted,
   skinned, cut into 4 cm (1½ in) pieces
3 egg yolks

Preheat the oven to 160°C (315°F/
Gas 2–3). To make croutons, brush
the bread with oil and then bake for
10 minutes. Rub with garlic. To make
the aïoli, put egg yolks, garlic and
3 teaspoons of lemon juice in mortar
and pestle and pound until creamy.
Add oil, whisking constantly, then add
in a thin, steady stream. Season and
add lemon juice. Refrigerate.

To make the stock, soak saffron in
1 tablespoon of hot water for about
15 minutes. Put saffron, wine, leek,
carrot, onion, orange zest, the fennel
seeds, thyme and fish trimmings in a
saucepan with 1 litre (35 fl oz/4 cups)
water. Cover and bring to the boil.
Simmer for 20 minutes then strain into
a saucepan. Bring to a simmer, add
half the fish and poach for 5 minutes.
Remove. Cook rest of fish. Remove
from pan. Bring stock back to the boil
and boil for 5 minutes.

Put half the aïoli and the yolks in a
bowl and mix until smooth. Whisk in
a ladleful of hot stock, then bit by bit
add 5 ladlefuls, stirring constantly.
Pour back into pan, whisk over low
heat for 3–5 minutes, or until hot and
thickened slightly. Season. To serve,
put the croutons in a bowl with a few
pieces of fish and ladle soup over top.

Serves 4

Tunisian fish soup

60 ml (2 fl oz/¼ cup) olive oil
1 chopped onion
1 chopped celery stalk
4 crushed garlic cloves
2 tablespoons tomato paste
  (concentrated purée)
1½ teaspoons ground turmeric
1½ teaspoons ground cumin
2 teaspoons harissa
1 litre (35 fl oz/4 cups) fish stock
2 bay leaves
200 g (7 oz/1 cup) orzo or other small
  pasta
500 g (1 lb 2 oz) mixed skinned
  snapper and sea bass fillets, cut
  into bite-sized chunks
2 tablespoons chopped mint
2 tablespoons lemon juice

Heat the olive oil in a large saucepan, add the onion and celery stalk. Cook for 8–10 minutes, or until softened. Add the garlic cloves and cook for a further minute. Stir in the tomato paste, turmeric, cumin and harissa and cook, stirring constantly, for 30 seconds.

Pour the fish stock into the saucepan and add the bay leaves. Bring to the boil, then reduce the heat to low and simmer gently for 15 minutes. Add the orzo and cook for about 10 minutes, or until *al dente*.

Add the fish. Poach gently for about 3–4 minutes, or until opaque.

Stir in the chopped mint and lemon juice. Season to taste. Garnish with a few extra mint leaves, if desired.

Serves 6

Smoked fish chowder

500 ml (17 fl oz/2 cups) milk
500 g (1 lb 2 oz) smoked fish,
  trimmed and cut into large chunks
50 g (1³/₄ oz) butter
1 leek, white part only, roughly
  chopped
2 celery stalks, chopped
1 large carrot, chopped
2 garlic cloves, chopped
400 g (14 oz) potatoes, cut into 5 cm
  (2 inch) pieces
1 teaspoon freshly grated nutmeg
500 ml (17 fl oz/2 cups) chicken stock
  or fish stock
125 ml (4 fl oz/¹/₂ cup) cream
1 large handful flat-leaf (Italian)
  parsley, chopped

Heat milk in a large deep saucepan. Add fish and simmer for 8 minutes, or until flesh flakes when tested. Transfer fish to a plate and set aside to cool. Reserve milk. Peel and discard skin from fish and roughly flake the flesh, removing any bones.

Heat butter in a large heavy-based saucepan over medium–low heat. Add leek, celery, carrot and garlic. Stir for 2 minutes to coat vegetables in the butter. Reduce the heat, cover and sweat, stirring occasionally, for 5 minutes. Do not allow the vegetables to brown.

Add chopped potato and nutmeg to the saucepan and stir. Cook for 2 minutes, then add stock. Bring to the boil, cover and cook for 20 minutes, or until the potato is tender. Set aside to cool slightly.

Using an immersion blender fitted with chopping blade, whizz soup for 10 seconds, or until roughly puréed. Stir in fish, reserved milk, cream and parsley and gently reheat the soup. Season well black pepper.

Serves 4–6

Prawn laksa

1 kg (2 lb) raw prawns
80 ml (2½ fl oz/⅓ cup) oil
2–6 small fresh red chillies, seeded
1 onion, roughly chopped
3 garlic cloves, halved
2 cm x 2 cm (¾ in x ¾ in) piece fresh
  ginger or galangal, chopped
3 lemongrass stems, white part only,
  chopped
1 teaspoon ground turmeric
1 tablespoon ground coriander
2 teaspoons shrimp paste
625 ml (21½ fl oz/2½ cups) coconut
  cream
2 teaspoons grated palm sugar or
  soft brown sugar
4 kaffir lime leaves, crushed
1–2 tablespoons fish sauce
200 g (7 oz) packet fish balls
190 g (6¾ oz) packet fried tofu puffs
250 g (9 oz) dried rice vermicelli
125 g (4½ oz) bean sprouts
20 g (¾ oz) chopped mint
2 teaspoons coriander (cilantro)
  leaves

Peel prawns and gently pull out dark vein from each, starting at the head end. Reserve heads, shells and tails. Cover and refrigerate prawn meat. Heat 2 tablespoons of oil in a wok or saucepan and add the prawn shells and heads. Stir over medium heat for 10 minutes, or until orange, then add 1 litre water. Bring to the boil, reduce the heat and simmer for 15 minutes. Strain the stock through a sieve and discard shells. Clean pan.

Finely chop the chillies, onion, garlic, ginger and lemon grass with turmeric, coriander and 60 ml (2 fl oz/¼ cup) of the prawn stock in a food processor.

Heat the rest of the oil in pan, add chilli mixture and shrimp paste, and stir over medium heat for 3 minutes. Pour in remaining stock and simmer for 10 minutes. Add the lime leaves coconut cream, sugar and fish sauce, and simmer for 5 minutes. Add the prawns and simmer for 2 minutes, or until light pink. Add fish balls and tofu puffs and simmer gently until heated through. Soak rice vermicelli in boiling water for 2 minutes, drain and divide it among the serving bowls. Top with bean sprouts and ladle soup over top. Sprinkle with mint and coriander.

Serves 4

Zuppa di pesce

Fish stock
300 g (10½ oz) firm white fish fillets,
    such as red mullet or cod, skinned
    and cut into cubes, bones reserved
12 prawns (shrimp)
1 small onion, roughly chopped
1 carrot, roughly chopped
15 g (½ oz) parsley, roughly chopped,
    stalks reserved

200 g (7 oz) squid tubes
4 tablespoons olive oil
1 onion, finely chopped
1 celery stalk, finely chopped
1 carrot, finely chopped
2 garlic cloves, finely chopped
pinch of cayenne pepper
1 fennel bulb, trimmed and sliced
125 ml (4 fl oz/½ cup) dry white wine
400 g (14 oz) tinned chopped
    tomatoes
250 g (9 oz) scallops, cleaned

Crostini
3 tablespoons extra virgin olive oil
2 garlic cloves, crushed
4 slices country-style bread

To make fish stock, rinse fish bones in water. Peel and devein prawns and put fish bones and prawn shells in a saucepan with just enough water to cover. Bring slowly to a simmer. Add onion, carrot and stalks from parsley, then simmer for 20 minutes. Strain through a colander and measure out 1.5 litres (52 fl oz/6 cups) stock.

Lie squid out flat, skin side up, and score a crisscross pattern into flesh. Slice diagonally into bite-sized strips.

Heat oil in a saucepan and cook the onion, celery, carrot, garlic and the parsley over low heat for 5–6 minutes. Add cayenne pepper and season. Stir in fennel and cook for 2–3 minutes. Add white wine, increase the heat and cook until absorbed. Stir in tomatoes, then add the fish stock and bring to the boil. Reduce the heat and simmer for 20 minutes.

Add squid to pan with fish pieces and simmer for 1 minute. Add the scallops and prawns and simmer for a further 2 minutes. To make crostini, heat olive oil and garlic in a frying pan over low heat. Add slices of bread and fry on both sides until golden. Place a slice of bread into each serving bowl. Ladle soup on top and serve immediately.

Serves 4

Fish soup

2 red capsicums (peppers)
1 long red chilli
2 tablespoons extra virgin olive oil
1 onion, finely chopped
1 tablespoon tomato paste
  (concentrated purée)
2–3 teaspoons harissa, to taste
4 garlic cloves, finely chopped
2 teaspoons ground cumin
750 ml (26 fl oz/3 cups) fish stock
400 g (14 oz) tinned crushed
  tomatoes
750 g (1 lb 10 oz) firm white fish, such
  as blue eye cod or ling, cut into
  2 cm (3/4 in) cubes
2 bay leaves
2 tablespoons coriander (cilantro)
  chopped leaves

Cut the capsicums into quarters and remove the membrane and seeds. Cut the chilli in half and remove the seeds. Place the capsicum and chilli skin side up under a hot grill (broiler) and grill (broil) until the skin blackens. Remove and place in a plastic bag, tuck the end of the bag underneath and leave to steam until cool enough to handle. Remove the skin, cut the flesh into thin strips and reserve.

Heat the oil in a large saucepan and cook the onion for 5 minutes, or until softened. Stir in the tomato paste, harissa, garlic, cumin and 125 ml (4 fl oz/1/2 cup) water. Add the stock, tomatoes and 500 ml (17 fl oz/2 cups) water. Bring to the boil, then reduce the heat and add the fish and bay leaves. Simmer for 7–8 minutes.

Remove the fish and discard the bay leaves. When the soup has cooled slightly, add half the coriander and purée until smooth. Season with salt and pepper. Return the soup to the pan, add the fish, capsicum and chilli and simmer gently for 5 minutes. Garnish with the remaining coriander and serve hot with crusty bread.

Serves 6

Marmite dieppoise

300 g (10½ oz) salmon fillet, skinned
400 g (14 oz) sole fillet, skinned
455 ml (16 fl oz) cider or
  dry white wine
16 mussels, cleaned
50 g (1¾ oz) butter
1 garlic clove, crushed
2 French shallots, finely chopped
2 stalks celery, finely chopped
1 large leek, white part only, thinly
  sliced
250 g (9 oz) small chestnut
  mushrooms, sliced
12 large raw prawns (shrimp), peeled
  and deveined
1 bay leaf
300 ml (10½ fl oz) thick cream
3 tablespoons flat-leaf (Italian) parsley,
  finely chopped

Cut the salmon fillet into bite-sized chunks and cut the sole into thick strips widthways. Set aside. Pour the cider or white wine into a saucepan and bring to a simmer. Add mussels, cover, and cook for 3–5 minutes, shaking pan every now and then. Put a fine sieve over a large bowl and tip mussels into sieve. Transfer mussels to a plate, throwing away any that haven't opened during cooking. Line the sieve with muslin and strain the cooking liquid again to get rid of any grit or sand.

Add butter to the cleaned saucepan and melt over medium heat. Add the garlic, shallot, celery and leek and cook, stirring, for 7–10 minutes, or until vegetables are just soft. Add the mushrooms. Cook for 4–5 minutes, or until softened. While vegetables are cooking, remove mussels from shells.

Add strained cooking liquid and bay leaf to vegetables in saucepan and bring to a simmer. Add the salmon, sole and the prawns and cook for 3–4 minutes, or until fish is opaque and prawns are pink. Stir in the cream and the cooked mussels and simmer gently for 2 minutes. Season to taste and stir in parsley.

Serves 6

Lobster soup with zucchini and avocado

50 g (1³/₄ oz) butter
1 garlic clove, crushed
2 French shallots, finely chopped
1 onion, chopped
1 zucchini (courgette), diced
2¹/₂ tablespoons dry white wine
400 ml (14 fl oz) fish stock
250 g (9 oz) cooked lobster meat, chopped
250 ml (9 fl oz/1 cup) thick cream
1 avocado, diced
1 tablespoon coriander (cilantro) leaves, chopped
1 tablespoon parsley, chopped
lemon juice, to serve

Melt the butter in a large saucepan. Add the garlic, chopped shallots, onion and zucchini and cook over medium heat for 8–10 minutes, or until the vegetables are just soft.

Add the wine and bring to the boil, keeping it on the boil for 3 minutes. Pour in the stock and bring to the boil again. Reduce the heat to low, add the lobster and simmer for 1–2 minnutes, until warmed through. Gently stir in the cream. Season with salt and freshly ground black pepper.

Ladle the soup into 4 bowls and stir a little avocado, coriander and parsley into each one. Squeeze a little lemon juice over the soup.

Serves 4

Clam chowder

30 g (1 oz) butter
2 bacon slices, finely chopped
1 large onion, finely chopped
4 potatoes, cut into small cubes
500 ml (17 fl oz/2 cups) fish stock
1 bay leaf
125 ml (4 fl oz/$1/2$ cup) milk
4 x 105 g (3$1/2$ oz) tins baby clams,
   drained and chopped
15 g ($1/2$ oz) finely chopped parsley
250 ml (9 fl oz/1 cup) cream

Heat butter in a large saucepan.
Cook the bacon and onion for
2–3 minutes, or until softened.
Stir in potato. Cook for another
2–3 minutes, then gradually pour
on the stock. Add the bay leaf.

Bring the mixture to the boil, then
reduce the heat and simmer, covered,
for 20 minutes, or until the potato is
cooked. Simmer for 10 minutes, or
until the soup is reduced and slightly
thickened. Discard the bay leaf.

Add the milk, chopped clams, parsley
and cream. Stir to reheat, but do not
allow the soup to boil. Season with
salt and freshly ground black pepper.

Serves 4

Zarzuela

Sofrito base
2 large tomatoes, peeled
1 tablespoon olive oil
2 onions, finely chopped
1 tablespoon tomato paste
  (concentrated purée)

Picada
3 slices white bread, crusts removed
1 tablespoon almonds, roasted
3 garlic cloves
1 tablespoon olive oil
1 raw lobster tail (about 400 g (14 oz)
750 g (1 lb 10 oz) firm white fish
  fillets, such as cod, cut into pieces
plain (all-purpose) flour for coating
2–3 tablespoons olive oil
125 g (4^1/$_2$ oz) squid tubes, cleaned
  and cut into rings
12 raw large prawns (shrimp)
125 ml (4 fl oz/^{1}/$_2$ cup) dry white wine
12–15 black mussels, cleaned
125 ml (4 fl oz/^{1}/$_2$ cup) brandy
3 tablespoons chopped parsley

Score a cross in base of tomatoes. Cover with boiling water. Leave for 30 seconds then cover with cold water and peel. Cut each tomato in half and scoop out seeds. Chop flesh. To make sofrito, heat the oil in a large flameproof casserole dish onstovetop. Add onion and stir for 5 minutes. Add the tomato, tomato paste and 125 ml (4 fl oz/^{1}/$_2$ cup) water and then stir for 10 minutes. Stir in 125 ml (4 fl oz/ ^{1}/$_2$ cup) water. Season.

To make picada, finely chop bread, almonds and garlic. Stirring, gradually add oil to form a paste. Preheat oven to 180°C (350°F/Gas 4). Cut lobster tail into rounds and set aside. Season flour and coat fish. Heat oil in a frying pan and fry fish pieces over medium heat for 2– 3 minutes. Add them to the casserole dish.

Add the squid and cook, stirring, for 1–2 minutes. Cook the lobster and prawns for 2–3 minutes. Add both to the casserole. Add wine to pan and bring to the boil. Add mussels, cover and steam for 4–5 minutes and add to casserole. Pour brandy into same pan, ignite and let flames die down before pouring over seafood. Mix, cover and bake for 20 minutes. Stir in picada and cook for 10 minutes.

Serves 4–6

Hot and sour prawn soup

350 g (12 oz) raw prawns (shrimp)
1 tablespoon oil
3 lemongrass stalks, white part only,
   bruised
3 thin slices of galangal
2 litres (70 fl oz/8 cups) chicken stock
or water
5–7 bird's eye chillies, stems
   removed, bruised
5 kaffir lime leaves, torn
2 tablespoons fish sauce
70 g (2 oz) straw mushrooms, or
   quartered button mushrooms
2 spring onions (scallions), sliced
3 tablespoons lime juice
a few coriander (cilantro) leaves,
   to garnish

Peel and devein the prawns, leaving tails intact and reserving heads and shells. Heat the oil in a large stockpot or wok and add the prawn heads and shells. Cook for 5 minutes or until the shells turn bright orange.

Add one stalk of lemongrass to the pan with the galangal and stock or water. Bring to the boil, then reduce the heat and simmer for 20 minutes. Strain the stock and return to the pan. Discard the shells and flavourings.

Finely slice the remaining lemongrass and add it to liquid with chillies, lime leaves, fish sauce, mushrooms and the spring onions. Cook gently for 2 minutes.

Add the prawns and cook for about 3 minutes or until the prawns are firm and pink. Take off the heat and add the lime juice. Taste, then adjust the seasoning with extra lime juice or fish sauce if necessary. Garnish with coriander leaves.

Serves 4

Seafood stews

Hot and sour fish stew

Spice paste
2 lemongrass stems, white part only,
cut into three pieces
1 teaspoon ground turmeric
a small knob fresh galangal or ginger
3 small red chillies
1 large garlic clove, peeled
4 red Asian shallots, peeled
1 teaspoon shrimp paste
60 ml (2 fl oz/¼ cup) oil
½ small red capsicum (pepper), thinly
sliced into strips
3 tablespoons tamarind purée or
lemon juice
1 tablespoon fish sauce
2 teaspoons grated palm sugar
225 g (8 oz) canned sliced bamboo
shoots, drained
500 g (1 lb 2 oz) pomfret fillets,
skinned, cut into bite-sized pieces
2 tablespoons coriander (cilantro)
leaves, chopped
1 tablespoon mint, chopped
steamed rice, to serve

To make the spice paste, put all the
ingredients in a food processor and
process to a paste. Alternatively, finely
chop all ingredients and mix together
by hand.

Heat the oil in a saucepan and add
the spice paste. Cook for 10 minutes,
stirring. Add the capsicum strips and
cook for a further minute. Add 750 ml
(26 fl oz/3 cups) water, the tamarind,
fish sauce, sugar and ½ teaspoon
salt and bring to the boil.

Reduce the heat to low and simmer
for 5 minutes, then add the bamboo
shoots and fish pieces and poach the
fish gently for 3–4 minutes, or until
opaque. Stir in the coriander and mint
and serve over plenty of steamed rice.

Serves 4

Stuffed squid stew

100 ml (3½ fl oz) olive oil
1 large onion, finely chopped
2 garlic cloves, crushed
80 g (2¾ oz/1 cup) fresh
  breadcrumbs
1 egg, lightly beaten
60 g (2¼ oz) kefalotyri cheese, grated
60 g (2¼ oz) haloumi cheese, grated
4 large or 8 small squid (about 1 kg/
  2 lb 4 oz), cleaned
1 small onion, finely chopped, extra
2 garlic cloves, crushed, extra
500 g (1 lb) firm ripe tomatoes, peeled
  and diced
150 ml (5 fl oz) red wine
1 tablespoon chopped oregano
1 tablespoon chopped flat-leaf (Italian)
  parsley

Heat 2 tablespoons of the oil in a frying pan, add the onion and cook over medium heat for 3 minutes. Remove. Combine with the garlic, breadcrumbs, egg and cheese. Season well.

Pat the squid hoods dry with paper towels and, using a teaspoon, fill them three-quarters full with stuffing. Do not pack them too tightly or the stuffing mixture will swell and burst out during cooking. Secure the ends with wooden toothpicks.

Heat remaining oil in a large frying pan, add the squid and cook for 1–2 minutes on all sides. Remove. Add the extra onion and cook over medium heat for 3 minutes, or until soft, then add the extra garlic and cook for a further 1 minute. Stir in tomato and wine, and simmer for 10 minutes, or until thick and pulpy, then stir in the oregano and parsley. Return squid to the pan and cook, covered, for 20–25 minutes, or until tender. Serve warm with the tomato sauce or cool with a salad.

Serves 4

Ligurian fish stew

Fish stock
250 g (9 oz) red snapper fillet, cut into
    chunks, bones reserved
250 g (9 oz) cod or turbot fillet, cut
    into chunks, bones reserved
250 g (9 oz) monkfish fillet, cut into
    chunks, bones reserved
6 large prawns (shrimp)
1 small onion, roughly chopped
1 carrot, roughly chopped
15 g (1/2 oz) flat-leaf (Italian) parsley,
    roughly chopped, stalks reserved

125 ml (4 fl oz/1/2 cup) olive oil
1 red onion, halved and thinly sliced
1 large fennel bulb, thinly sliced
3 garlic cloves, thinly sliced
800 g (1 lb 12 oz) tinned tomatoes
310 ml (10¾ fl oz/1¼ cups) dry white
    vermouth or wine
large pinch of saffron threads
450 g (1 lb) waxy potatoes, quartered
    lengthways
450 g (1 lb) mussels

To make fish stock, rinse fish bones
in cold water. Peel and devein prawns
and put them and prawn shells in a
saucepan with water to cover. Bring
to a simmer. Add onion, carrot and
stalks from parsley, then simmer for
20 minutes. Strain through a sieve
and measure 1 litre (35 fl oz/4 cups)
stock. To make soup base, heat oil in
a saucepan and cook the onion and
fennel for 5 minutes. Add garlic and
tomatoes. Bring to the boil, reduce
heat and simmer until reduced to a
thick sauce. Add 200 ml (7 fl oz) of
vermouth, saffron and the potatoes.
Increase the heat and boil for about
5 minutes, add fish stock, reduce the
heat and simmer for 10 minutes, or
until potatoes are cooked.

Scrub mussels, pull off beards and
discard any broken or cracked ones.
Bring remaining vermouth to the boil
in another saucepan, add the mussels
and cover and cook for 1 minute, or
until shells open. Remove mussels
from shells and place in a bowl. Pour
over cooking liquid, discarding any
sediment in pan. Add prawns and the
fish to soup. Stir briefly, season and
then simmer for 5 minutes, until fish is
cooked. Add mussels to reheat, then
leave for 10 minutes before serving.
Add parsley and serve with bread

Serves 6

Catalan fish stew

300 g (10½ oz) red mullet fillets
400 g (14 oz) firm white fish fillets
300 g (10½ oz) cleaned calamari
1.5 litres (52 fl oz/6 cups) fish stock
80 ml (2½ cup fl oz/⅓ cup) olive oil
1 onion, chopped
6 garlic cloves, chopped
1 small fresh red chilli, chopped
1 teaspoon paprika
pinch saffron threads
150 ml (5 fl oz) white wine
425 g (14 oz) tinned crushed
  tomatoes
16 raw prawns, peeled and deveined,
  tails intact
2 tablespoons brandy
24 black mussels, cleaned
1 tablespoon chopped parsley

Picada
2 tablespoons olive oil
2 slices day-old bread, cubed
2 garlic cloves
5 blanched almonds, toasted
2 tablespoons flat-leaf (Italian)
parsley

Cut the fish and calamari into 4 cm
(1½ in) pieces. Place stock in a large
saucepan, bring to the boil and then
boil for 15 minutes, or until reduced
by half. To make the picada, heat oil
in a frying pan, add bread and then
cook, stirring, for 2–3 minutes, or until
golden, adding the garlic for the last
minute. Place almonds, bread, garlic
and parsley in a food processor and
process, adding stock to make a
smooth paste. Heat 2 tablespoons of
oil in a large saucepan, add the onion,
the garlic, chilli and paprika, and then
cook, stirring, for 1 minute. Add the
saffron, wine, tomato and stock. Bring
to the boil, reduce heat and simmer.

Heat the remaining oil in a frying pan
and quickly fry fish and calamari for
3–5 minutes. Remove from the pan.
Add prawns, cook for 1 minute and
then pour in brandy. Carefully ignite
brandy with a match and let flames
burn down. Remove from pan. Add
mussels to stock and then simmer,
covered, for 2–3 minutes, or until
opened. Discard any mussels that do
not open. Add all the seafood and the
picada to pan, stirring until the sauce
has thickened. Season to taste and
sprinkle with parsley to serve.

Serves 6–8

Suquet de peix

1 tablespoon olive oil
1 carrot, finely diced
1 onion, finely diced
1 leek, finely diced
3 garlic cloves, chopped
1 small red chilli, seeded and finely
  chopped
1 celery stalk, finely diced
2 large potatoes, cut into 2 cm
  ($^3/_4$ in) dice
500 g (1 lb 2 oz) firm white fish fillets,
  cut into 2 cm ($^3/_4$ in) dice, reserving
  any bones and scraps
1 bay leaf
250 ml (9 fl oz/1 cup) white wine
30 ml (1 fl oz) brandy
400 g (14 oz) tinned diced tomatoes,
  drained
60 g (2$^1/_4$ oz/$^1/_4$ cup) tomato paste
  (concentrated purée)
12 mussels, debearded and scrubbed
8 raw king prawns (shrimp), peeled
  and tails removed
2 tablespoons lemon juice
2 tablespoons flat-leaf (Italian) parsley,
  chopped

Heat the oil in a large saucepan over medium heat. Add carrot, onion, leek, garlic, chilli and celery and then cook for 5 minutes, or until the onion is translucent. Add potato and 1.5 litres (52 fl oz/6 cups) cold water. Bring to the boil, then reduce heat and simmer for 8 minutes, or until potato is semi-cooked. Stir in fish bones and scraps and bay leaf and simmer for about 6–8 minutes, or until potato is soft. Strain liquid and reserve. Remove the bones, scraps and the bay leaf, and then purée the remaining potato and vegetable mixture with reserved liquid.

In a separate saucepan, combine wine, brandy, tomato paste and diced tomato and bring to the boil. Add the mussels and then cook, covered, for 3 minutes, or until opened. Remove from pan, discarding any mussels that remain closed.

Stir the mussel liquid into the potato purée. Transfer to a large saucepan and bring to the boil. Add fish pieces and prawns, reduce heat and simmer for 8 minutes, or until all the seafood is cooked.

Stir in the mussels and lemon juice and gently heat through. Season well and garnish with the parsley.

Serves 4–6

Mexican seafood stew with avocado salsa

60 ml (2 fl oz/¼ cup) olive oil
1 large onion, chopped
1 large stalk celery, chopped
3 garlic cloves, crushed
2 small thin red chillies, seeded and
  finely chopped
200 ml (7 fl oz) fish stock
800 g (1 lb 12 oz) tinned roma (plum)
  tomatoes
2 bay leaves
1 teaspoon dried oregano
1 teaspoon caster (superfine) sugar
2 large cobs corn, kernels removed
500 g (1 lb 2 oz) halibut fillets,
  skinned
2 tablespoons chopped coriander
  (cilantro) leaves
juice of 2 limes
12 raw tiger prawns (shrimp), peeled
  and deveined, tails intact
8 scallops
12 clams, cleaned
125 ml (4 fl oz/½ cup) thick cream

Avocado salsa
½ small avocado
½ small red onion, finely chopped
1 tablespoon coriander (cilantro)
  leaves, chopped
1 lime finely grated, zest and juice

Heat oil in a large saucepan. Add the onion and celery and cook over a medium–low heat for 10 minutes, stirring. Add the garlic and the chillies and then cook for 1 minute, stirring.

Add fish stock and the tomatoes and break the tomatoes up in pan. Stir in bay leaves, oregano and sugar and bring to the boil. Allow to bubble for 2 minutes, then reduce the heat to low and gently simmer for 10 minutes. Allow to cool for 5 minutes, remove the bay leaves and tip mixture into a food processor and whizz until fairly smooth, but still retaining texture.

Return mixture to pan and season. Add corn kernels and bring back to the boil. Reduce heat and cook for 3 minutes. Cut fish into chunks. Stir in coriander and lime juice, add the fish, then simmer gently for 1 minute. Add prawns and scallops and scatter the clams on top. Cover with a lid and cook for 2–3 minutes, or until seafood is opaque and clams steam open.

Chop avocado into small cubes and mix with red onion, coriander and lime zest and juice. Season. Stir cream into stew, ladle into bowls and serve with salsa.

Serves 4

Provençal seafood stew with fennel

4 tablespoons extra virgin olive oil
1 large onion, finely chopped
1 bulb fennel, trimmed and finely
  chopped
2 garlic cloves, chopped
2 thyme sprigs
pinch chilli flakes
grated zest of ½ orange
3 tablespoons Pernod
400 g (14 oz) tinned tomatoes
300 ml (10½ fl oz) fish stock
½ teaspoon saffron threads
250 g (9 oz) ling fillet
250 g (9 oz) swordfish steak
12 large raw prawns (shrimp)
25 g (1 oz/¼ cup) pitted black olives,
  chopped
2 tablespoons chopped parsley
cooked tagliatelle, to serve

Heat oil in a sauté pan and fry onion, fennel, garlic, thyme, chilli flakes and orange zest for 5 minutes, or until softened and lightly golden. Add the Pernod, bring to the boil and cook for 2–3 minutes, or until reduced by half.

Stir in tomatoes, stock and saffron. Bring to the boil, cover and simmer for 30 minutes, or until the sauce is thickened slightly.

Meanwhile, prepare the seafood. Cut the ling and swordfish into large chunks. Peel the prawns and using a small knife, cut down the back of each one, pull out and discard the black intestinal tract and wash well. Pat the prawns dry on paper towel.

Add e seafood to the stew with the olives and parsley, return to the boil and cook for 5–10 minutes, or until the seafood is tender. Season with salt to taste. Rest for 5 minutes and serve the stew with the cooked tagliatelle, tossed with a little olive oil, if desired.

Serves 4

Octopus in red wine stew

1 kg (2 lb 4 oz) baby octopus
2 tablespoons olive oil
1 large onion, chopped
3 garlic cloves, crushed
1 bay leaf
750 ml (26 fl oz/3 cups) red wine
60 ml (2 fl oz/¼ cup) red wine vinegar
400 g (14 oz) tinned crushed
   tomatoes
1 tablespoon tomato paste
   (concentrated purée)
1 tablespoon finely chopped oregano
¼ teaspoon ground cinnamon
small pinch ground cloves
1 teaspoon sugar
2 tablespoons chopped flat-leaf
   (Italian) parsley

To prepare each octopus, take a small knife and cut between the head and tentacles, just below the eyes. Grasp the body and push the beak out and up through the centre of the tentacles with your fingers. Cut the eyes from the head by slicing a small round off with a small sharp knife. Discard the eye section. Carefully slit through one side of head and remove any gut from inside. Rinse octopus thoroughly under running water.

Heat oil in a large saucepan, add the onion and cook over a high heat for 5 minutes, or until starting to brown. Add the garlic and bay leaf and cook for another minute. Add the octopus and stir to thoroughly coat in the onion mixture.

Add the wine, vinegar, tomato, tomato paste, oregano, cinnamon, cloves and sugar. Bring to the boil, then reduce the heat to low and simmer for 1 hour, or until octopus is tender and sauce has thickened slightly. Stir in parsley and season.

Serves 4–6

Caruru

350 g (12 oz) tomatoes
1 tablespoon dried shrimp
3 tablespoons oil
1 onion, chopped
1 small green capsicum (pepper),
  seeded and chopped
1 green chilli, finely chopped
3 garlic cloves, crushed
3 tablespoons crunchy peanut butter
400 ml (14 fl oz) coconut milk
100 g (3½ oz) small okra, topped and
  tailed
½ teaspoon paprika
600 g (1 lb 5 oz) cod fillet, skinned
3 tablespoons coriander (cilantro),
  chopped

Score a cross in the base of each tomato. Plunge into boiling water for 20 seconds, then drain and peel the skin away from the cross. Chop the tomatoes, discarding the cores and seeds.

Put the dried shrimps in a small bowl, cover with boiling water and leave to soak for 10 minutes, then drain. Heat the oil in a deep-sided frying pan. Add onion and green capsicum and cook for 5 minutes, stirring every now and again. Add chilli and garlic and cook for a further 2 minutes, stirring. Add chopped tomato and its juices, peanut butter, coconut milk, the okra, paprika and the dried shrimp. Bring the mixture to the boil, then reduce the heat to medium and simmer for 12–15 minutes, or until okra are soft.

Meanwhile, cut cod into large chunks. Add fish to the pan, stir and simmer gently to cook. Test after 3 minutes; if cod flakes easily, it is ready. Season and scatter coriander over the top.

Serves 4

Moqueca de peixe

4 x 200 g (7 oz) fish steaks such as
mahi mahi, bream or halibut
8 raw large prawns (shrimp), peeled
and deveined
60 ml (2 fl oz/¼ cup) lime juice
2 tablespoons olive oil
1 large onion, finely chopped
4 large cloves garlic, crushed
1 large red capsicum (pepper),
seeded and chopped
1 habañero chilli, seeded and finely
chopped
500 g (1 lb 2 oz) vine-ripened
tomatoes
300 ml (10½ fl oz) coconut milk
3 tablespoons coriander (cilantro)
leaves, chopped

Put the fish and prawns in a shallow
non-metallic dish. Drizzle the lime
juice over the seafood. Season and
turn the fish in the juice. Cover and
refrigerate for 30 minutes.

Meanwhile, heat the oil in a large
saucepan and add the onion. Cook
for 8–10 minutes, until softened. Add
the garlic, capsicum and chilli and
cook for a further 3 minutes, stirring
occasionally. Score a cross in the
base of each tomato. Put into boiling
water for 20 seconds, then plunge
into cold water. Drain and peel the
skin away from the cross. Chop the
tomatoes, discarding the cores and
seeds. Add the tomato to the pan
and cook for 10 minutes.

Allow to cool slightly, then tip sauce
into a food processor or blender and
whizz until smooth. Alternatively, push
the mixture through a coarse sieve or
mouli by hand. Return the sauce to
the pan. Add the coconut milk and
bring to a gentle simmer. Lift the fish
and the prawns out of the dish and
add to the pan, leaving behind any of
the remaining marinade. Cook for
4 minutes or until opaque. Season to
taste with salt and black pepper and
sprinkle the coriander over the top.

Serves 4

Stocks

There's nothing quite like homemade soup. It's enjoyable and surprisingly easy to make if you follow a few commonsense rules, and can be dressed up or down to suit just about any occasion.

Stock secrets

While soup is ideal for using up odds and ends from the refrigerator, it is only as good as its ingredients, and the backbone of any good soup is its stock. There are several alternatives when choosing stock. You can use home-made, fresh or frozen stock available from some delicatessens or poultry shops, or tetra packs or cubes from the supermarket. The best stock will be home-made or fresh and, as it can be frozen, it is a good idea to cook up large quantities every time. Tetra packs are convenient, as are stock cubes; however, check the labels and choose cubes made from natural ingredients with no added MSG. Commercial stocks always tend to be much saltier than home-made, so taste the soup before seasoning with salt and pepper. Always season soup at the end of the cooking time, as long cooking concentrates the flavours.

Try to use the flavour stock called for in the recipe. A beef stock would be overpowering in a recipe that calls for chicken stock, although vegetarians might prefer to use vegetable stock in all their soups.

Purée and strain

Many soups are puréed before serving and there is a sensible way to go about this. Let the soup cool a little first, so that it is safe if it splashes. Cool it quickly by pouring it into a bowl, then wash the pan to take the puréed soup for reheating. Purée in either a food processor or a blender — a blender will give a finer result, though it tends to aerate the soup slightly. Always purée in batches, never filling the processor above halfway.

Occasionally, recipes ask for the soup to be strained, particularly if making the stock is part of the recipe. A fine sieve (not a colander) is usually adequate. Some clear soups need more than one straining through a sieve lined with damp muslin. If you don't have muslin, use a clean damp kitchen cloth.

Ahead of time

Many soups can be made in advance and do, in fact, benefit from overnight refrigeration as the flavours develop. Use commonsense to determine if any of the ingredients will not store well, for example if the soup has cream, add it when you are reheating for serving. The same goes for pasta; for instance, if you add the pasta to minestrone, then leave it to sit around, it will be unpleasantly soggy. Generally, soups can be kept for up to 3 days in the refrigerator, or frozen in airtight containers or freezer bags for up to 1–3 months. A lot of soups become very thick on standing and need to be diluted when reheated. Use more of the same stock, water or cream, as appropriate. The seasoning will also need to be adjusted.

Most recipes call for a heavy-based pan for making soup. This is so that the pan distributes heat evenly and prevents anything 'catching' on the bottom. A wide, shallow pan will allow too much evaporation. The recipe will state if the pan should be covered. If it is not to be covered the soup will simmer and, as the liquid evaporates off it, it will reduce down and thicken. So, if your soup is still a little thin, simply simmer it uncovered for a while. Most soups are cooked at a gentle simmer, meaning that the surface of the soup is barely moving, while a simmer means the soup will be moving faster but without bubbles breaking the surface. Boiling is when bubbles actively break the surface of the soup. Watch the soup and adjust the heat accordingly. If the recipe says to partially cover the pan, tilt the lid at an angle so that there is a gap for steam to escape.

Soup is a dish whose sum is definitely greater than its parts. And one of its most important parts is stock. A good stock makes the difference between an ordinary and a spectacular soup, giving full-bodied flavours and a sound base for the other ingredients. If you are looking at these recipes and thinking the cooking times seeming very long and it all looks like too much trouble, think again. It doesn't take long to chop up the ingredients and then you can leave your stock to simmer lazily while you get on with other things.

Home-made versus ready-made

The flavour of soup is improved by using home-made stock, plus you know exactly what ingredients have gone into your dish. If possible, make stock a day in advance and store it in the fridge. This will improve the flavour and you'll find the fat solidifies on top and can be easily lifted off with a spoon.

How to make perfect stock

* Stock can be made from raw or cooked meat and poultry, but fish stock should be made from raw non-oily fish.

* The quality of stock depends on the type of bones that you use — marrow bones, pigs' trotters and chicken wings will produce a jellied stock (when cold) as they contain collagen.

* Vegetables should be aromatics (leek, onion, carrot, celery), as should herbs (bay leaves, thyme and parsley). For clear stock, use whole spices such as black peppercorns rather than ground pepper. Vegetables that give off starch, such as potatoes, will turn your stock cloudy.

* Stock must be simmered for a long time (although not as long for fish) and never boiled — boiled stock becomes cloudy and greasy as the fat is incorporated into the liquid.

* As your stock simmers, skim off any scum that rises to the surface. To bring scum (fat and impurities) to the surface, add a little cold water at regular

Beef stock

Roast 1.5 kg (3 lb 5 oz) beef or veal bones in a single layer in a large roasting tin at 220°C (425°F/Gas 7) for 20 minutes. Do not burn the bones or your stock will be bitter.

Add 1 quartered onion, 2 chopped carrots, 1 chopped leek and 1 chopped celery stalk and roast for a further 20 minutes.

Transfer to a stockpot along with 10 peppercorns and a bouquet garni. Cover with 4 litres (16 cups) of cold water and bring to the boil.

When the stock boils, turn it down to a simmer and skim off the scum.

Skim regularly — adding a little cold water to the pot will help any of the impurities rise up to the surface so they can be skimmed off. After 6–8 hours, strain the stock and leave it to cool in the fridge. When cool, lift off any congealed fat.

Chicken stock

Put 1 kg (2 lb 4 oz) chicken carcasses into a stockpot with a bouquet garni, 1 quartered onion, 1 chopped carrot and 10 peppercorns.

Add 4 litres (16 cups) cold water and bring to the boil. When the stock boils, turn it down to a simmer and skim off the scum.

Skim regularly — adding a little cold water to the pot will help any impurities rise up to the surface so they can be lifted off.

Strain the stock and remove any fat by dragging a sheet of paper towel over the stock surface.

If not using immediately, cool in the fridge. When cool, lift off any of the congealed fat.

Once made, a stock can be reduced (by boiling) for freezing. The stock can then be poured into ice cube trays and frozen. Reconstitute with water before use. Store the stock in the fridge for up to 3 days, or frozen for up to 6 months.

Fish stock

Put 2 kg (4 lb 8 oz) fish bones and heads in a stockpot with a bouquet garni, 1 chopped onion and 10 peppercorns.

Add 2.5 litres (10 cups) cold water, bring to the boil and then simmer for 20–30 minutes. Skim off any scum.

Strain the stock, then cool in the fridge. When cool, lift off any congealed fat.

Vegetable stock

Put 500 g (1 lb 2 oz) mixed chopped carrots, celery, onions and leeks in a stockpot. Add a bouquet garni and 10 peppercorns.

Add 2.5 litres (10 cups) cold water, bring to the boil and then simmer for 1–2 hours. Skim off any scum that arises on surface regularly.

Press solids to extract all the flavour, then strain and cool in the fridge.

Index

INDEX

INDEX

INDEX

Published in 2010 by Murdoch Books Pty Limited

Murdoch Books Australia
Pier 8/9, 23 Hickson Road
Millers Point NSW 2000
Phone: +61 (0)2 8220 2000
Fax: +61 (0)2 8220 2558
www.murdochbooks.com.au

Murdoch Books UK Limited
Erico House, 6th Floor
93–99 Upper Richmond Road
Putney, London SW15 2TG
Phone: +44 (0)20 8785 5995
Fax: +44 (0)20 8785 5985
www.murdochbooks.co.uk

Chief Executive: Juliet Rogers

Publisher: Lynn Lewis
Senior Designer: Heather Menzies
Photography (cover): Stuart Scott
Stylist (cover): Louise Bickle
Editorial Coordinator: Liz Malcolm
Production: Kita George

National Library of Australia Cataloguing-in-Publication Data
Title: Soups and Stews. ISBN: 978-1-74196-952-8 (pbk.)
Series: Chunky series. Subjects: Soups. Stews. Dewey Number: 641.813

Printed by 1010 Printing International.
PRINTED IN CHINA

Cover credits: Orange side plate & tea cup, pale blue bowl and plate, Mud Australia.
Blue spot fabric, orange stripe fabric, floral print fabric, No Chintz.

IMPORTANT: Those who might be at risk from the effects of salmonella poisoning (the elderly,
pregnant women, young children and those suffering from immune deficiency diseases) should
consult their doctor with any concerns about eating raw eggs.

OVEN GUIDE: You may find cooking times vary depending on the oven you are using. For fan-
forced ovens, as a general rule, set the oven temperature to 20°C (35°F) lower than indicated
in the recipe.